Journeys to Heaven and to Hell

Journeys to Heaven and to Hell

RODNEY DAVIES

ROBERT HALE · LONDON

© *Rodney Davies 2002*
First published in Great Britain 2002

ISBN 0 7090 6986 3

Robert Hale Limited
Clerkenwell House
Clerkenwell Green
London EC1R 0HT

The right of Rodney Davies to be identified as
author of this work has been asserted by him
in accordance with the Copyright, Design and
Patents Act 1988.

A catalogue record for this book is available from the British Library

2 4 6 8 10 9 7 5 3 1

Typeset in 11/13 pt Garamond
by Derek Doyle & Associates, Liverpool.
Printed by
St Edmundsbury Press Limited, Bury St Edmunds
and bound by
Woolnough Bookbinding Limited, Irthlingborough

The evening wind is sad with farewells,
And loving hands unclasp from mine;
Alone I go to meet the darkness
Across an awful boundary line.

As from the lighted hearths behind me
I pass with slow, reluctant feet,
What waits me in the land of strangeness?
What face shall smile, what voice shall greet?

What space shall awe, what brightness blind me?
What thunder-roll of music stun?
What vast processions sweep before me
Of shapes unknown beneath the sun?

From *What the Traveller Said at Sunset*
by John Greenleaf Whittier

Contents

Acknowledgements

I thank the British Library, where some of my research was done, and also two Finchley booksellers, Martin Gladman and Michael Songhurst, from whom a number of helpful out-of-print works were obtained. Special thanks go to Peter Wood for allowing me to reproduce part of his privately communicated series of 'dreams', and to Bloynan of the Near-Death and Other Worlds' Association for letting me publish passages from his NDE, the entirety of which can be read at *www.ndowa.com*. I am also most grateful to Mitchell Berger, Professor of Mathematics at University College, London, who kindly explained how to calculate the time it would take for an object to fall down a tunnel to the centre of the earth, and to Shirley Jenkins for her help in not only identifying the source of a poetry quotation but for the care she once took in teaching me how to write 'good English'.

Extracts from the copyright material shown below are kindly reprinted by permission of the publishers.

Oxford University Press: *The Apocryphal New Testament*, translated by Montague Rhodes James. The Penguin Group (UK): *History of the English Church and People* by Bede, translated by Leo Sherley-Price; *Concerning the City of God Against the Pagans* by St Augustine, translated by Henry Bettenson, *The Epic of Gilgamesh*, translated by N.K. Sandars; *The Histories* by Herodotus, translated by Aubrey de Selincourt; and *The Republic* by Plato, translated by Desmond Lee. *Telegraph Magazine*: testimony of Mary Errington from 'Life After Death – Are We Closer to the Truth?' by Mick Brown, 27 March 1993. HarperCollins

Publishers: *Memories, Dreams, Reflections* by Carl Jung, translated by Richard and Clara Winston. Elsevier Science: *The Lancet*, 3 September 1983, pp. 561–2, 'A Near-Death Experience' by I.R. Judson and E. Wiltshaw.

However, despite every effort being made to contact all authors or publishers of copyright material, this has proved impossible in some cases. My apologies are offered to those concerned.

1

Body and Soul

There is no people, rude or learned, among whom apparitions of the dead are not related and believed. This opinion, which perhaps prevails as far as human nature is diffused, could become universal only by its truth.

From *The History of Rasselas* by Dr Samuel Johnson

The belief that there is some form of existence after death is very ancient. Evidence for this is revealed by ancient grave sites, the earliest of which date back about 10,000 years, whose occupants were not only interred with care but were often laid to rest along with food, wine and various utensils which they might require in the next world. Tribal leaders, and later emperors and kings, as well as others of high rank, were also often buried with a representative selection of their servants, concubines and horses, which had been specially killed for the occasion and whose services they were thought to need in order to live as comfortably in death as they had in life.

But our ancestors did not think the physical body itself entered the next realm, except in the sense that burial banished it to a dark, dank recess in the earth. This is confirmed by the alternate and widespread practice of cremation, whereby the body is reduced to ashes. Rather, they supposed that that which the living physical body had contained, its inner or true self, went on to, and thereafter persisted in, the underworld. This elusive, mysterious entity was both the life force which animated the person during life and the essence of his or her

11

personality and capabilities. As this was normally unseen and apparently without substance, it became known to English speakers as a 'spirit', from the Latin *spiritus*, meaning 'breath' – hence 'the breath of life' – as well as a 'ghost' or a 'wraith', both of which derive from northern European words for the life force. Today it is commonly called the 'soul', whose Greek equivalent *psyche* forms the subject of such word compounds as 'psychology' and 'psychiatry'.

There are occasions, however, when this mysterious inner self becomes visible, which typically happens soon after a person dies. It then reveals itself to be an exact likeness of him or her, including clothing, although its overall colouring is generally somewhat paler. And curiously, it still retains an ability to impinge upon its surroundings and also to speak, which indicates that it is both quasi-physical and conscious. Sometimes the likeness leaves the body when it is asleep or in a trance, and when this happens it may be seen at a place where the physical self is not.

The separated likeness or simulacrum is traditionally called a 'double' or, to use the German term, a *doppelgänger*, meaning 'double-goer', although when seen either shortly before or after death, it is known as a 'wraith'. The numerous witnessed accounts from all over the world of a double or a wraith indicate that it is a genuine supernatural phenomenon. Sightings are so frequent that they cannot simply be explained away as mistaken identity, coincidental similarity, tricks of the light or deliberate imposture.

A beautiful description of a wraith was recorded in *De anima* by the Carthage-born Latin Church father Quintus Tertullian (AD 160–230). A Christian convert, Tertullian did much to promote early Church unity but became increasingly alienated by its worldliness, which prompted him to join the Montanists, an ecstatical and heretical sect whose members claimed to receive revelations directly from the Holy Spirit.

One female Montanist who often saw visions during their Sunday services once told Tertullian that 'among other things there was shown to me a soul in bodily form, and it appeared like a spirit; but it was no mere something, void of qualities, but rather a thing which could be grasped, soft and translucent, and of etherial [sic] colour, in form at all points human.'

When the double leaves someone's body, perhaps to manifest at a distant location, he or she is effectively in two places at the same time, a phenomenon known as 'bilocation'. Furthermore, if this happens during sleep, the consciousness may accompany the double, which enables the person to view the world through its eyes. And when it returns to the sleeper, he or she upon waking typically interprets whatever was seen or experienced as a dream.

Although the double is sometimes referred to as an 'apparition of the living', it is nevertheless not the same as a ghost. We have already noted that it has a quasi-physical nature, which the ghost lacks. This allows the double to reflect light and thus to appear entirely solid and lifelike, unlike the typical ghost which is semi-transparent. Indeed, the double has sufficient 'substance' to prevent it from passing through closed doors, walls and other solid barriers, through which the diaphanous ghost can travel without hindrance. However, the double can also manifest as if by magic from out of thin air, often at a place many miles from its source, and thereafter vanish from view in the same astonishing way. Yet because the double is on occasions seen by one person but not by those with him or her, psychic sensitivity may play a role in its apprehension.

Moreover, a ghost usually performs the same actions at the same place and often at the same time. These purposeless repetitions constitute a haunting. Such characteristics together suggest that a ghost is little more than a hazy remnant of a dead person, usually a murder victim or suicide, and lacks both consciousness and independence. It is therefore probably the exterior layer of a departed wraith, which was excoriated from its surface by the negative emotions of rage, jealousy, hate, depression or despair that led to the person's demise. And these, by persisting at the murder site, hold the ghostly remnant *in situ* and thereafter cause it to repeat the same actions over and over again, much like images projected from a continuously running loop of film. However, as time passes, the negative energies gradually weaken and dissipate, and the ghost thereby appears less frequently and less visibly, until both they and it fade away completely. This explains why the oldest ghosts date back to only Elizabethan times and why most are far more recent.

A fascinating account of wraiths was given by Elizabeth Hobson, a 24-year-old woman from Sunderland, County Durham, to John Wesley (1703–91), the founder of Methodism, when he interviewed her over a three-day period in May 1768. She began by telling him:

From my childhood, when any of our neighbours died, whether men, women, or children, I used to see them either just when they died or a little before. And I was not frightened at all it was so common. Indeed many times I did not then know they were dead. I saw many of them by day, many by night. Those that came when it was dark, brought light with them. I observed all little children and many grown persons had a bright, glorious light round them. But many had a gloomy dismal light, and a dusky cloud over them.

Elizabeth, an orphan, went on to say that when she was sixteen years old her beloved uncle and guardian Thomas Rea died, which broke her heart. Her grief so weakened her that she began to deteriorate physically. Then one night, after having shed many tears and seemingly having prayed in vain for a visit from him, his wraith came into her bedroom, although he looked, she said, 'much displeased, shook his head at me, and in a minute or two went away'.

Elizabeth's condition continued to worsen during the following two weeks, and her carers thought that her end was near. But then her uncle's wraith visited her again late one evening, and sat down beside her on the bed. This time, she noted, he appeared 'well pleased'. His nocturnal visits thereafter became more frequent, cheering her up considerably and thus playing a part in her subsequent recovery.

He came every night after at the same time, and stayed till cock-crowing. I was exceeding glad, and kept my eyes fixt upon him, all the time he stayed. If I wanted drink or any thing, though I did not speak or stir, he fetched it, and set it on the chair by the bedside. Indeed, I could not speak; many times I strove, but could not move my tongue. Every morning when he went away he waved his hand to me, and I heard delightful music, as if many persons were singing together.

Hence Thomas Rea's wraith was not only an exact likeness of himself when alive, but it had sufficient solidity and motive power to walk around and to lift and move glasses and other solid objects with apparent ease. And notwithstanding the fact that it did not speak to Elizabeth, the wraith was clearly conscious and had the ability to divine her needs and desires, perhaps by telepathy. Indeed, the wraith was in all respects just as much alive as the physical Thomas had been, thereby indicating that while his dead body had been buried, the inner man – or perhaps, as we might call him, the real man – continued to exist after death in the same form that he had possessed in life.

Buoyed up by the visits of Uncle Thomas's wraith, Elizabeth began slowly to get better and in six weeks she was more or less back to normal. Then one evening her deceased guardian called on her again. This proved to be his last visit. He was dressed differently and was later joined by another otherworldly figure, who seemed to be an angelic companion and/or guide. The description of both accords with what others have experienced at such times.

He came in, and stood by the bedside. But he was not in his usual dress: he had on a white robe which reached down to his feet. He looked quite well pleased. About one, there stood by him a person in white, taller than him and exceedingly beautiful. He came with the singing as of many voices, and continued till near cock-crow-ing. Then my uncle smiled and waved his hand towards me twice or thrice. They went away with inexpressible sweet music, and I saw him no more.

15

The length of time that Thomas Rea's wraith remained in this world was unusual, and evidently only happened because of his great concern for the life of his niece. The wraith is really the equivalent of an escape vehicle, providing consciousness with a familiar boundary and setting in which it can be taken to, and function in, the next realm of being. How long it remains there will be discussed later, but it does mean that when we first travel to the next world we can expect to meet others in their familiar form, with whom we can interact as normal, thus experiencing life there much as we have done in this world.

I have had one encounter with a visible wraith, which was made even more interesting by the fact that the meeting took place between the wraith and my exteriorized double while I was asleep, and thus resembled, in that regard, a dream, although its quality was far more intense than a dream. And remarkably, the wraith I met, which was that of my aunt, was clad in a long white robe much like that worn by the wraith of Thomas Rea. This in turn suggests, if the incident actually happened, that it was her final visit to this world.

My aunt died after a long illness in November 1999. She had long been interested in psychic matters, and had sparked my interest in the field as a child. In fact this book, like most of my others, owes much to her influence. We had often discussed the possibility that some form of existence continues after death, and I recall her once saying to me that she would, if possible, visit me from beyond the grave. She fulfilled that pledge, or so I believe, almost exactly two months after she died. This is what happened:

At about 1 a.m. on Saturday, 19 January 2000, while fast asleep in bed, I dreamt that I was sitting working at my writing table. The time was obviously late as it was dark outside, just as it was in actuality. Then the telephone rang and I heard my elderly mother answer it, and not long afterwards she called out that Peggy was on the line and wanted to speak to me. I hurried to the telephone, but found to my surprise that the receiver had been replaced. Thinking that my mother had become confused, I turned back and, to my utter astonishment, saw Peggy coming up the nearby stairs. Not only did she look about twenty years younger, but she was wearing a long white robe, which reached down to her ankles and had a distinct pad on each shoulder, ¬ather like a narrow epaulette, with serrated sides, and from which the robe seemed to hang.

When she gained the landing, I threw my arms around her in delight, exclaiming how marvellous it was to see her again. But while she both looked and felt entirely solid and real, I was desperately trying to work out how she could be there. I was sure that she had died, but here she was alive again! It then occurred to me that, like the people I had written about in my recently published book entitled *Buried Alive*, she must have been wrongly certified as dead, but had somehow recovered and then been rescued from her coffin before her cremation.

This 'insight' woke me with a start and I found myself back in bed, where another shock awaited me. For upon opening my eyes in the darkness of my bedroom, I saw hovering in the air just above my shins a white, cloud-like mass. It was 2 or 3 feet in diameter and about 9 inches thick, and it was gently undulating somewhat in the manner of a large pond amoeba.

I had never seen such a manifestation before, but after gazing at it for several seconds I shut my eyes to it, trying to take in the wonder of seeing my aunt. When I opened them again, the unusual cloud was still there. I watched its strange movements, feeling a mixture of apprehension and incredulity, quite sure that it had its origin in my aunt. Its presence seemed to confirm that what I had seen while asleep was not a dream image but her wraith, which I had encountered while briefly out of my body in my double form. Then feeling suddenly tired, I laid my head back on the pillow and before I knew it I was asleep. When I awoke the next morning the cloud had vanished.

The meeting with my aunt, although it occurred during sleep, was far more vivid and compelling than a dream. The encounter also happened in my home, which ordinarily I never dream about. And my aunt, in addition to looking much younger, wore an outfit that I could never have imagined her wearing. She had been quite a stylish dresser in life and would not, if you'll excuse the expression, have been seen dead wearing a long white robe with narrow wavy epaulettes!

Taken together, these features correspond sufficiently well with the experiences of those who have had a double-separation while asleep to suggest that I underwent the same thing, and that it was actually caused by my aunt visiting me from the next world. And her short sojourn there, I'm pleased to report, had done her good, because not only did she look younger and more glamorous and healthy than she had in her later years, but she was able to climb, without evident effort, a flight of stairs which would previously have been impossible for her, owing to hip replacements and osteo-arthritis.

St Augustine, in *Concerning the City of God Against the Pagans*, states, 'I believe that a person has a phantom which in his imagination or in his dreams takes on various forms ... [and it] can in some inexplicable fashion be presented in bodily form to the apprehension of other people.' And he quotes the following interesting example of the surprise appearance of a sleeper's double:

Another man reported that in his own house, at night-time, before he went to bed, he saw a philosopher coming to him, a man he knew very well; and this man explained to him a number of points in Plato, which he had formerly refused to explain when asked. Now this philosopher was asked why he had done something in the other's house which he had refused to do when requested in his own home, and he said in reply, 'I did not do it; I merely dreamed that I did.' This shows that what one man saw in his sleep was displayed to the other, while awake, by means of a phantom appearance.

However, a double or wraith is not simply a three dimensional representation of the outer form of a person, like a hologram. It also has a replicated internal structure, and in this regard is a true duplicate, which enables it to function much as does or did the physical person, notwithstanding it has certain unconventional abilities. Thus it apparently possesses enhanced psychic powers and it can materialize out of thin air and fade away equally astonishingly. The double sometimes, and the wraith always, contains the person's consciousness, which makes it aware of its surroundings, and it can also speak by exhaling air through its duplicate larynx and by refining the sound waves with its replicated tongue, cheeks and lips. And while Thomas Rea's wraith, like my aunt's, did not speak, there have been many reports over the years of wraiths that have been talkative to the point of volubility, despite the fact that they are usually laconic.

About one year after Elizabeth Hobson lost her uncle, a good friend of hers named John Simpson was drowned at sea. His wraith not only began visiting her shortly afterwards, wet with the brine of his watery grave, but it eventually spoke to her at some length. At first he visited her once in the night between eleven and two o'clock – 'Before he came and when he went away, I always heard sweet music,' Elizabeth noted – but a week later he started calling on her three times during the day as well, at sunrise, at noon, and at sunset. It took Elizabeth a little while to summon up sufficient courage to speak to the returned wraith, but when she finally managed to ask him why he came, he told her that he could find no rest until she had kept the promise she had given him to look after his children when he died. He then helpfully advised her not to travel to Jamaica to join her brother, or to marry, as both would be detrimental to her welfare.

John Simpson's wraith also made some brief comments about the next world. These were given when Elizabeth expressed a wish to die, which prompted John to tell her that her time had not yet come, although he added: 'And yet, if you knew as much as I do, you would not care how soon you died.' And when she asked him how he spent his time in the next world, he replied: 'In songs of praise. But of this you will know more by and by: for where I am, you will surely be. I

19

have lost much happiness by coming to you. And I should not have stayed so long without using other means to make you speak: but the Lord would not suffer me to fright you.'

When Elizabeth was afterwards visited by the wraith of John Hobson, her deceased grandfather, whom she calls 'an exceeding wicked man', his vocalization was of a more complex, unconventional character: 'His voice was loud, and so hollow and deep, that every word went through me. His lips did not move at all (nor his eyes), but the sound seemed to rise out of the floor. When he had done speaking, he turned about, and walked out of the room.'

On another occasion Elizabeth's grandfather frightened her by his expostulations at her mentioning God, causing her to reach out to the Lord in her heart, whereupon 'he gave a shriek, and sunk down three times, with a loud groan at each time. Just as he disappeared, there was a large flash of fire, and I fainted away.' Her dead relative's wickedness was also revealed by the fact that whenever he visited her late at night and her bedroom was in darkness, 'as soon as he came, all the room was light, but with a dismal light, like flaming brimstone'.

The classic modern example of a double being seen while the person concerned was asleep happened in the last decade of the nineteenth century. It was related by the traveller and author Augustus Hare (1834–1903) in his autobiography, which is straightforwardly entitled *The Story of My Life*. The strange incident was told him by a Miss Broke, the niece of the country-dwelling friends with whom he stayed in November 1894.

Miss Broke said that a few years earlier an Englishwoman named Butler, who lived with her wealthy husband in Ireland, had one night had a vivid dream in which she found herself rambling around a lovely country house, whose interior and surroundings so impressed her that she excitedly told her husband about it in the morning, saying:

Last night I had the most wonderful night. I seemed to be spending hours in the most delightful place, in the most enchanting house I ever saw – not large, you know, but just the sort of house one might live in one's-self, and oh! so perfectly, so deliciously comfortable. Then there was the loveliest conservatory, and the garden was so enchanting. I wonder if anything half so perfect can really exist.

The next day she told her bemused husband that she had again dreamed of visiting the same house, this time adding: 'I sat in the library: I walked on the terrace; I examined all the bedrooms: and it is simply the most perfect house in the world.' Mrs Butler thereafter often spoke of exploring the delightful house in her dreams, and it became something of a commonplace for a time to be asked by her husband and any guests at breakfast if she had been there the night before, although gradually other matters claimed their attention.

In 1892, when the Butlers finally tired of the insolence and ingratitude of the native Irish and returned to England, they took temporary accommodation in London while searching for a suitable property to buy within a 40-mile radius of the capital. None seemed suitable, until at last they went to look at a house in Hampshire, which had a surprisingly low price. When they arrived at its lodge Mrs Butler was astonished to recognize both it and the drive beyond as belonging to the house in her dreams, and her excitement mounted when she saw the house itself. 'But this is my house!' she exclaimed, and then promptly flummoxed the housekeeper by conducting her around it. Yet Mrs Butler's biggest surprise occurred when, after they had bought the property, she and her spouse called on the agent to ask why it was so modestly priced. Augustus Hare continued:

The agent had started violently when they came in, but recovered himself. Then he said to Mrs Butler, 'Yes, it is quite true the matter is quite settled, so there can be no harm in telling now. The fact is the house has had a great reputation for being haunted; but you, madam, need be under no apprehensions, for you are yourself the ghost!'

21

This is a wonderful tale, although it is regrettable that it was told to Augustus Hare by Miss Broke and not by Mrs Butler. Indeed, we must wonder why Mr Hare did not afterwards try to contact the Butlers to determine if what he had heard was true. But if it is, then it can only mean that Mrs Butler left her body while asleep and visited the house in question in her double form, where her frequent and visible appearances frightened its owners, who took her for a ghost and hurriedly sold the property for a knock-down price!

A somewhat similar and equally remarkable case was reported to me by the man to whom it happened, Peter Wood of Silverdale, Lancashire. It is further evidence that the double or 'second self' can leave the sleeping physical body and travel to another location, and perhaps into the presence of another person, who may or may not be able to see it.

Peter, who is now in his late fifties, said that he began having several different types of dream at the age of twelve, following the death of his father. Most of them, however, 'either came to a conclusion or faded away' as he got older, although there was one which stayed with him for many years. Its subject, a young girl, gradually grew into an adult in the dream, so giving Peter the unique opportunity to watch her mature and experience the different events of her life.

In the beginning, whilst I was a teenager, I was like a fly on the wall. I saw this young woman studying at school, going home, doing various chores around the house, playing the piano – sometimes playing pieces I played, but [she] was more proficient and more ahead of me . . . Over the years I never gave much thought to these incidents but as time went on the 'visits' to this person became stronger. I felt I was standing by her when she was practising, washing up. She got married and in my 20s I found I could talk to her and at first she seemed to hear me but couldn't speak – then she answered me and we had conversations like someone on the telephone, speaking but not seeing.

The young woman in the dream eventually began to study

music in Manchester, and Peter said, 'I saw various scores that I did not know when "awake". I identified two later on. One was by Zipoli, another was a piece in E minor by Buxtehude, which had special significance for her.' But despite the regularity of his apparent visits to the young woman while he slept, Peter had no idea that his experiences were anything other than dreams with a common theme, remarking, 'All these things I thought were pure imagination as it was in dreams. When we are asleep so is everyone else, but what happened was in daytime.'

The dreams continued at intervals throughout Peter's twenties and thirties, with sometimes months between them. And strangely, the woman continued to age in step with the passage of time. Indeed, Peter witnessed her marriage and the birth of her three children, and he remarked, that 'I saw her three children grow up. Pete (the eldest) and Kirsty (the youngest) twigged our conversations. The middle child I did not know and is just a vague figure. There were so many incidents but I did not tell anyone then.' Yet two events did occur which are relevant to what I said above about the differences between doubles and ghosts. 'When I was about thirty-four or so I paid a visit – she was washing up and a black figure passed via the garden. It came through the house. She said, "Was it you?" I said, "No, it must be a ghost," and felt frightened. I woke up!'

Five years later, the woman's marriage broke down and she moved house, although the change of residence was anything but beneficial. Peter noted: 'She was very unhappy. She worried about the children who weren't with her. An old woman often sat in a chair near her. She never moved or said anything and was "misty". I assumed it was a ghost and said nothing to her.'

During this period, Peter, who for some time had been heard by the woman, also became visible to her, which meant he was able to interact with her fully in the way that one ordinarily can with 'dream' images, as he still thought her to be. He also began relating his strange experiences whilst asleep to

friends and colleagues, none of whom knew what to make of
them. But then came the drama of what turned out to be his
last visit to her, which alerted him to the fact that his nocturnal adventures were something more than a series of
connected dreams. He said: 'Then my last visit occurred. I
went to her as normal. By then she could see me as well as
speaking. She was very cross and said, "This is the end. My
husband has died. I don't want to see you any more – go
away!" I woke up with such a start and was very upset.'

This incident prompted Peter to discuss the matter with his
vicar, who was only able to tell him, 'There are a lot of things
in the subconscious, like a jigsaw that will not fit. There is no
answer.' However, Peter began to wonder increasingly if the
woman was a real person, and eventually remembered that
when he was a child of five he had known two girls at his
primary school, named Margaret R. and Marion R. (unre-
lated), and that one day they had together all pricked their
fingers and mingled their blood to give them a special bond.
With the help of a former journalist on the *Northern Echo and
Yorkshire Post* Peter discovered that Margaret had been killed
many years before in a car crash, and that the father of Marion
now worked for the Christadelphian Church. Indeed, Peter
eventually learned that all Marion's family were
Christadelphians, which is why he now believes he lost
contact with her after he left primary school, as his father
disapproved of the sect. He next wrote to Marion's father at
the church, and in due course received a reply from her
mother, who invited him to visit her. When they met, she
shocked him by saying, 'I asked you here because Marion
died of leukaemia when she was thirty-nine and this date is
the anniversary of her death.' The unexpected announcement
rendered Peter speechless. But what happened next astounded
him.

Then I was shown a picture of Marion, but she was nothing like I
remembered her at school, the child who cried on her first day at
school and was my closest friend there. *The picture was of the*

woman I had dreamed about all those years [author's italics]. I could say nothing . . .The rest of the conversation went over me. I was thinking about other things. I mourned her passing and wondered where I had visited her. The address was correct, even though I had never been to Prestbury physically. Then another shock. Peter and Kirsty were real people – two of the three children – and the very day I had been told to 'Go away' by Marion was the day before her husband had remarried, against the rules of the Christadelphian Church.

This is a truly remarkable case, although it is admittedly difficult to understand how Peter, who dreamed of being with Marion when he was asleep at night, invariably seemed to visit her in what appeared to be the daytime, when she was awake. He should instead have found himself in her house when she was either going to bed or lying in bed, as happened to the sleeping philosopher's double who called on a man to expound some points in Plato with him, which he had previously refused to do. But it may mean that the double can shift somewhat backwards or forwards in time, and thereby be with another when he or she is awake. And although this may sound suspect, I would urge sceptical readers to consider the case of Peter Ackroyd, described in *Doubles: The Enigma of the Second Self*, who when he was asleep one night in 1996 suddenly found himself in an early eighteenth-century street and then in a house in the year 1858.

By separating itself from the sleeping body, the double can, as the above cases make plain, visit places to which the individual concerned could not normally go to when awake and there speak to and physically interact with other people. Indeed sometimes very naughty things may be done by a wandering double, when it acts out the darker sexual desires of its lower self. One of the most shocking examples of sexual depravity performed by a sleeping man's double was described by Lewes Lavertus of Tigurine in his book entitled *Of Ghosts and Spirites, Walking by Night*, published in 1596. He wrote:

I

I heard of a grave and wise man, which was a Magistrate in the Territorie of *Tigurine*, who affirmed, that as he and his servant went through the pastures, in summer very early, he espied one whome he knew very well, wickedly defiling himself with a Mare, wherewith being amazed, he returned back again, and knocked at his house, whome he supposed he had seen, and there understood for a certaintie, that he went not forth out of his chamber of morning. And in case he had not diligently searched out ye matter, the good and honest man had surely bin cast in prison, and put on the rack.

It is probable that the nocturnal activities of sexually predatory doubles gave rise to the folk belief in the incubus and succubus, the former supposedly being an evil male spirit and the latter an evil female spirit, which had intercourse with sleepers of the opposite sex during the night. The quasi-physical properties of the double make such activity possible, although only those people who can will their double to separate from their body, and whose morals are subservient to their sexual desires, would defile the bodies of unresisting sleepers. Witches and warlocks were once thought to perform such out-of-body indecencies, and it is probable that the numerous myths describing how a god or goddess slept with a mortal are based on them. The sleeping Endymion, for example, was supposedly carnally enjoyed by the moon-goddess Selene, and the similarly somnolent Psyche was penetrated by Cupid, the love god.

However, the separation of the double from the physical body has been more frequently attempted by those who wish either to ramble about in this world or to explore spiritual domains that would ordinarily be inaccessible to them. Such separation is most readily effected by entering a state of trance, and various techniques for becoming entranced were developed by primitive peoples, who hoped thereby to gain direct contact with, and assistance from, their gods. The most widespread and effective method of trance-inducement employed chanting, dancing, and repetitive drumming, which together helped to break down conscious mental controls and

throw the brain of the witch-doctor or shaman into a delightful type of spasm, known as ecstasy, during which his or her
double or soul body was believed to vacate its physical shell
and travel to the realm of the gods. Concerning these John
Potter (c.1674–1747), later Archbishop of Canterbury, wrote
in his *Archælogia Græca* (1698):

A third sort were the Exstatikos or those that were cast into Trances
or Ecstacies, in which they lay like men dead, or asleep, deprived of
all sense and motion; but after some time returning to themselves,
gave strange relations of what they had seen and heard. For it was
a vulgar opinion, that man's soul might leave the body, wander up
and down the world, visit the place of the deceased, and the heavenly regions, and by conversing with the gods and heroes, be
instructed in things necessary for the conduct of human life.

One of the earliest descriptions of a shaman inducing such
a trance is narrated by an English merchant adventurer named
Richard Johnson, who visited the Samoyeds, a nomadic
Mongol tribe living alongside the Perchere river in Siberia, in
January 1556. He noted:

First the Priest doth begin to play upon a thing like to a great sieve,
with a skin on the one end like a drum: and the stick that he played
with is about a span long, and one end is round like a ball,
covered with the skin of an Hart . . . Then he sings as we use here
in England to hallow, whoop, or shout at hounds, and the rest of
the company answer him with this 'Owtis, Igha, Igha, Igha', and
then the Priest replies again with his voices. And they answer him
with the selfsame words so many times, that in the end he becomes
as it were mad, and falling down as he were dead . . . I asked
them why he lay so, and they answered me, 'Now does our God
tell him what we shall do, and whither we shall go'. (Spelling
modernized)

The trance thus induced was often so deep that the shaman
or person concerned lost all awareness of his surroundings, to

the extent of not feeling pain, although the after-effects of an inflicted hurt were felt when he emerged from the trance. Indeed, St Augustine mentions the unusual case of a presbyter named Restitutus, who was able to 'deprive himself of all sense' whenever he wished, and who felt no pain at all when he was pricked, pinched or, as happened on one occasion, burned. And the French author Jean Bodin (c.1530–96), in *Le Theatre de la nature universelle*, comments wonderingly of the person lying rapt in an ecstatic trance, whose 'sleep is so profound . . . that he does not easily wake up when one lacerates him, and when one applies burning torches to his body'.

Yet few demonstrations of bodily numbness can be quite so remarkable as that exhibited by the above-mentioned Samoyed shaman, who having risen suddenly from the ground, took up a sword 'a cubit and a span [or about 2 feet] long', and then, according to the watching Richard Johnson,

put it into his belly halfway and sometime less, but no wound was to be seen, (they continuing in their sweet song still). Then he put the sword into the fire till it was warm, and so thrust it into the slit in his shirt and thrust it through his body, as I thought, in at his navel and out at his fundament: the point being out of his shirt behind. I laid my finger upon it, then he pulled out the sword and sat down.

The Samoyeds, in common with other northern European and Russian tribes, believed that the surface of the earth formed an interface between seven heavenly layers or strata above, which enclosed the world concentrically rather like the layers of an onion, and seven hellish ones below. Tangara, their chief benevolent deity, was thought to reside in the highest or seventh heaven, while different and less powerful benign deities occupied the other six layers, all of which tried to help mankind. A similar situation occurred below ground, where each subterranean layer was home to malignant gods, spirits and demons that were harmful to mankind, although Erlik Khan, the most evil of the underworld deities, lived in the fifth hellish layer. By visiting the upper layers the shaman's double would seek help or guidance from the benevolent gods, or conversely, by travelling to the underworld layers he would try to appease or repress the evil underworld deities that brought sickness, poor hunting and other ills.

The wandering of the exteriorized double in this world has been well documented, and I have described several instances in my earlier book on the subject. In the early thirteenth century, for example, the double of a German knight named Everadus Ambula visited Egypt, Lombardy and Rome, while his physical self apparently lay dead at home. On about 500 occasions in the early seventeenth century, while lying prone in an ecstatic trance at her convent in Agreda, Spain, the double of the Venerable Mary of Jesus was able to visit New Mexico and convert the heathen Jumano Indians. And one day in February 1855, the double of Alexander Ferguson, then an inmate at a secure lunatic asylum in Indianapolis, was seen walking among, shouting at, and drinking whisky before, his alarmed fellow townsfolk in New Harmony, which lies 150 miles south-west of the state capital.

A similar earth-bound wandering may be made by a wraith, and an interesting English example of this was described by William of Newburgh (c. 1135–c.1200) in his *Historia Rerum Anglicarum*. The incident was confirmed by Archdeacon Stephen of Buckinghamshire, where the incident happened, although all those who saw the man concerned believed him to have emerged somehow from his grave, and to be therefore one of the living dead.

The night following his burial on Holy Thursday (a moveable spring festival taking place one month after Easter), the man suddenly turned up at his home and climbed into bed with his horrified wife, lay on her, and nearly squashed her with his astonishingly increased post-mortem weight. When the same thing reoccurred the next night, it prompted the petrified woman, to call in some neighbours the following evening. They stood guard around the bed and drove off the man, when he arrived, by shouting at him. He thereupon directed his malevolent attention to his own brothers, but when they took similar counter-measures, he frightened the village animals with his presence. He next began turning up in the village during the daytime, when he demonstrated one particularly strange ability, which revealed that he was not in fact a wandering corpse but a wraith:

He began to wander abroad in daylight, formidable, indeed, but visible only to a few; for oftentimes, on his encountering a number of persons, he would appear to one or two only, though at the same time his presence was not concealed from the rest. At length the inhabitants, alarmed beyond measure, thought it advisable to seek counsel of the church; and they detailed the whole affair, with tearful lamentations, to the . . . archdeacon.

The archdeacon consulted the Bishop of Lincoln, then resident in London, about the matter, and the bishop, upon conducting a full enquiry which indicated that the unlikely event had actually happened, decreed that a letter of absolution be placed in the man's coffin, instead of burning his corpse as the villagers had wished. When the coffin was opened, the body showed no sign of having moved, but when it was reburied with the letter of absolution, the wandering wraith was never seen again, which suggests that it was at last able to leave this world for the next.

These remarkable occurrences together confirm my assertion that the physical body of every man and woman contains a replica self, which conforms to it in shape and which, during certain mental states like sleep or trance, may vacate it to visit either distant places or another realm of being. A similar separation often also occurs when someone clinically dies, when they have neither a detectable heartbeat nor a pulse, nor show other signs of life, but from which they are eventually resuscitated. It is at such times that the separated wraith may visit those regions which we call heaven and hell.

2

The Pagan Afterlife

Spirit, nearing yon dark portal at the limit of thy human state,
Fear not thou the hidden purpose of that Power which alone
   is great,
Nor the myriad world, His shadow, nor the silent Opener of
   the Gate.
      From *God and the Universe* by Alfred Lord Tennyson

Although most readers will probably be familiar with the
Christian belief in heaven and hell, which are two distinct
places where the dead supposedly reside, the former being
located somewhere in the sky and housing the good, the latter
lying deep beneath our feet and holding the bad, such
complete and polar separation of the dead on moral grounds
was unknown to those whom we call pagans (from *pagani*,
meaning 'country dwellers') or heathens (from *eidolon*, meaning 'idol', hence idol-worshipper), and who were distinguished by the fact that they worshipped many gods. Indeed,
the followers of the Old Religion thought that the dead all
went underground to the same dark realm, which was
presided over by the god and goddess of the dead.

There are several reasons for this. First, the sky, being made
up of air, seemed hardly substantial enough to support the
dead, let alone dwellings for them, and anyway it was too far
away to reach. The pagans also believed the vastness and over-
arching beauty of the sky identified it as divine and thus not a
suitable place for the souls of mere mortals, even though they
thought the gods only used it to fly or ride through, for they

31

lived – or so most pagans believed – on the summits of certain mountains. Hence despite the sky being called heaven, or Ouranos, the term was used in a more restricted sense for those particular mountain tops.

Thus to the ancient Greeks, the light, bright summit of Mount Olympus in Thessaly, the highest mountain in Greece, was considered to be the abode of their twelve principal deities, known collectively as the Olympians. It was thus the Greek heaven, although like most ancient peoples they regarded all mountains as holy places. Elsewhere, the pagan natives claimed that particular local mountain tops were the divine residences of their gods, to which human beings, whether dead or alive, were not invited, with occasional rare exceptions.

Some pagans, however, notably those living in Mesopotamia, whose night skies are particularly clear and bright, were more centred on the sky than on mountain tops, and they regarded the various celestial bodies which moved across it as deities. Hence heaven for them was primarily the sky. The Greeks also believed that the Sun, or Helius, and the Moon, or Selene, were deities, but they regarded them as being relatively low down in the order of command, which is perhaps why they did not develop the fixation with the gods of the firmament that was found among the inhabitants of the Tigris and Euphrates river valleys. Indeed, the latter peoples thought that each 'wandering star' or planet was the home of a deity, whose movement through the background of fixed stars, along with that of the Sun and the Moon, could be used to determine the destiny of their king and his kingdom, a practice now known as astrology. It was only towards the end of the first millennium BC that astrology was introduced by the Chaldeans into Greece and became at all popular.

The pagan underworld was pictured, in its earliest known form, as subterranean, dusty and forbidding, much like the interior of a grave or barrow, or indeed of a deep cave. In fact the Sumerians, who during the early third millennium BC built the first towns and cities in the delta region of the Tigris and

Euphrates rivers, have left us the first description of this dark realm, which surprisingly accords with some modern accounts of those who have visited, during a near-death experience (NDE), what they thought was hell.

The Sumerians, like many ancient peoples, believed that we all contain an identical interior self, which leaves the body at death and travels to the dark realm below. This wraith is clothed in replica habiliments, and is exactly like the physical person, being conscious and aware. Moreover, it is subject to the same restraints and limitations. The Sumerians also thought that its counterpart in life, the double, could leave the body during sleep, taking the consciousness of the sleeper with it, and visit distant places in this world, as well as sometimes the underworld. Then, when the person awoke, he or she would recall the out-of-body excursion as a dream.

One of the earliest and important Sumerian cities was Uruk, the Biblical Erech, whose fifth king, Gilgamesh, reigned there in about 2500 BC. Gilgamesh was evidently a remarkable man, for aside from building the first walls around Uruk, he was reputedly semi-divine (the son, it was said, of the goddess Ninsun) and his heroic exploits became the subject of the world's first heroic poem, known as the *Epic of Gilgamesh*. This work, with additions, eventually became the most popular saga, and Gilgamesh the most popular hero, throughout Mesopotamia, to the extent that it was still being recited or read until late in the first millennium BC, long after the Sumerians had ceased to exist as a separate people.

The poem begins by describing how Gilgamesh, the strongest man of his time, upset his male subjects by his unrestrained delight in copulating with their wives and daughters. Their complaints were heard by the gods, who resolved to create a man whose strength was equal to his and who would, by offering him a real manly challenge, thereby divert him from his life of unrestrained promiscuity.

The goddess Aruru accordingly made from clay his exact likeness, a hairy wild man named Enkidu, who at first lived at one with the animals of the woods and fields, but who eventually was tamed and civilized by six days and seven nights of passion spent with a specially commissioned harlot. Arriving in Uruk, Enkidu wrestled with, and was defeated by, Gilgamesh, but their combat proved to be such a deep bonding experience for the king that he fell into a state of intense brotherly love for the newcomer. Thereafter all Gilgamesh's thoughts and emotions were centred almost entirely on Enkidu, his 'second self', much to the relief of his cuckolded subjects.

However, following an expedition which Gilgamesh and Enkidu together made to the forest of Lebanon, where they killed Humbaba, its divine proprietor, Gilgamesh was wooed by Ishtar, the beautiful but inconstant goddess of love, who promised him all sorts of material rewards if he would marry her. But Gilgamesh, now an emotionally changed man, refused the goddess, not least perhaps because she was known to be notoriously unfaithful to her mortal lovers. Deeply angered by the slight, Ishtar persuaded Anu, the sky, to send down the Bull of Heaven to ravage the kingdom of Uruk. But Gilgamesh and Enkidu killed the Bull and thus saved Gilgamesh's realm, although Enkidu afterwards became seriously ill. And while he was asleep one night, he dreamed that he was carried to the underworld.

Enkidu's underworld journey was preceded by a loud roaring noise, similar to that which many, myself included, have heard while undergoing an out-of-body experience (such as may result from clinical death), and which indicates that it was probably based on a real one. This is also suggested by the fact that Enkidu's double was met by an underworld guide, a winged man-bird, who transformed him into a similar winged being. Such a startling double metamorphosis has not only been claimed by others, but the emergence of a bird from someone who is asleep or in a trance, while seemingly impossible, has been witnessed on numerous occasions. Indeed, I have described in *Doubles: The Enigma of the Second Self* how I once heard, while meditating, the unmistakable flapping sound of a bird's wings, as some mysterious entity, which was probably part of my double form, made two or three aerial circuits around my head. Enkidu said:

The heavens roared, and the earth rumbled back an answer; between them stood I before an awful being, the sombre-faced man-bird; he had directed me on his purpose. His was a vampire face, his foot was a lion's foot, his hand was an eagle's talon. He fell on me and his claws were in my hair, he held me fast and I smothered; then he transformed me so that my arms became wings covered with feathers.

Arriving thus transformed in the underworld, Enkidu found himself in an extremely dark and dismal place, which was very different from the hot, flame-filled hell of Christian ideology, but which was none the less curiously similar to that visited by some moderns:

He led me away to the palace of Irkalla, the Queen of Darkness, to the house from which none who enters ever returns, down the road from which there is no coming back. There is the house whose people sit in darkness; dust is their food and clay their meat. They are clothed like birds with wings for covering, they see no light, they sit in darkness.

Those confined in this unpleasant place were not punished for sins they had committed in life by being burned or tortured on racks; rather, their chastisement took the form of all being reduced to the same humble, desolate level, which naturally most affected those people who, while alive, took pride in their power, wealth and importance, like kings and princes. 'They who had stood in the place of the gods like Anu and Enlil, stood now like servants to fetch baked meats in the house of dust, to carry cooked meat and cold water from the water-skin.'

Enkidu's visit to the underworld ended shortly afterwards when, having encountered some of the dark realm's gods, he was recognized as an intruder by Belit-Sheri, their recorder, who demanded: 'Who brought this one here?' Her query woke Enkidu, presumably by sending his double form speeding back to his body.

Enkidu's remarkable experience is important because, as I have said, it contains several features that are found in many recent accounts of visits to the next realm, whether these were made to heaven or to hell. The most significant are: first, Enkidu was conducted below by a guide, who was winged, rather like a traditional Christian demon or angel; secondly, the underworld was reached by making a journey along a road; thirdly, he encountered wraiths of people there who had long since died; and fourthly, his presence was noticed by one who recognized him as being an interloper, in other words being there before his time. And equally significantly, the Sumerian underworld, like the modern hell, was a place of desolation and hopelessness, where those who were proud and arrogant in life suffered most by being reduced to an unending state of servitude.

In later times, the Mesopotamians pictured the underworld, which they named Kur, as being a vast, dark, mournful citadel surrounded by seven walls, each of which had a massive gate secured with seven bolts. An elderly gate-keeper named Neti (or Nedu) decided who was allowed in. Every admitted wraith or dead soul had to remove one item of clothing at each of the seven gates, making seven divestments in all, so that he or she came completely naked before the seven underworld judges or Anunnaki. The latter then decided what reward or punishment was merited. The exterior wall was also guarded by ugly, winged demons, who stopped anyone trying to escape. The ruler of Kur was the goddess Irkalla (also known as Ereshkigal), whose husband Nergal, the god of war, plague and pestilence, kept it well supplied with wraiths clamouring for admittance. Irkalla was the twin sister of Ishtar, the divine Queen of Heaven.

The close association made by the Sumerians and other Mesopotamians of seven with death, and likewise with rest, sleep, unconsciousness and peace, is thus an ancient one, and it is still recognized today in our week, for the seventh day is the day of rest. The Western week in fact originates from God's supposed creation of the world in six days as described in *Genesis*, following which he 'rested on the seventh day from all the work that he had made'. The Greeks, by contrast, identified death and the underworld with the number three.

The *Epic of Gilgamesh* also describes an earthly paradise which may have been the precursor of the biblical Garden of Eden, as well as one named Dilmun, which lay 'beyond the borders of death'. These are similar to the paradise visited by many more recent near-death victims, who subsequently found themselves, or so they believed, at the gates of heaven.

Enkidu's death following his 'dream' of the underworld not only broke Gilgamesh's heart, but it also brought home to him the fact that he too must soon die. He therefore resolved to seek out Utnapishtim, the Sumerian hero of the flood and the only man who had been granted immortality, from whom he hoped to learn the secret of eternal life. Gilgamesh's journey to reach Utnapishtim took him westward to the mountain of Mashu, through which he needed to pass to enter the garden of the setting sun. The gate to the mountain was guarded by the Scorpion-Men, who fortunately let him into the 36 mile long tunnel leading through the mountain.

This lengthy trek in itself is interesting, as Gilgamesh's passage occurred in complete darkness, until he finally emerged into the bright sunlight at its end. It is therefore similar to the tunnel-like journey terminating in a brilliant light often experienced by those undergoing a near-death experience. And the light revealed to Gilgamesh a divine garden:

There was the garden of the gods; all around him stood bushes bearing gems. Seeing it he went down at once, for there was fruit of carnelian with the vine hanging from it, beautiful to look at; lapis lazuli leaves hung thick with fruit, sweet to see. For thorns and thistles there were haematite and rare stones, agate, and pearls from out of the sea.

Gilgamesh next spoke with Shamash, the sun god, and with Siduri, the goddess of wine. The latter, on hearing of his quest, advised him to accept the inevitability of death and to eat, drink and be merry. But Gilgamesh refused to be deterred, whereupon Siduri said that to reach Utnapishtim he must traverse the ocean, the waters of death, which no living man had done before and which would require him to be ferried across by Urshanabi, the boatman of Utnapishtim.

After some delay and difficulty, Urshanabi and Gilgamesh finally reached Dilmun, the otherworldly paradise, where there was no sickness, old age, sorrow, cold or snow, or killing by wolves and lions, and where the immortal Utnapishtim happily resided with his wife. Indeed, it was the equivalent of heaven, despite the fact that it only contained two residents, both of whom were still alive.

Utnapishtim, the Mesopotamian Noah, recounted to Gilgamesh the story of the great flood and explained how he had saved the lives of himself and his family, and those of representative pairs of animals, by building a large, square-bottomed boat, following which narration he reluctantly imparted the secret of eternal life to Uruk's king. This entailed eating a certain thorny plant found growing at the bottom of the sea. Upon leaving Utnapishtim's paradise, Gilgamesh managed to retrieve this from the watery depths. Yet all did not end happily, for Gilgamesh delayed eating the plant and, when he slipped into an exhausted sleep beside a well, it was consumed by a snake, which accounts for the ability of these reptiles to rejuvenate themselves by shedding their skin. Returning to Uruk, the depressed, grief-stricken and worn out hero was told by the god Enlil that he should count the many blessings of life which had been given to him by the gods and accept that eternal life was not one of them. His counsel helped Gilgamesh come to terms with his mortality, which he held in common with all mankind, and he shortly thereafter died.

Thus while pagan Mesopotamians believed in the presence of a dark underworld below the earth, where all wraiths were sent following the death of their physical bodies, they also held that two divine earthly gardens existed, which, although not inhabited by human wraiths, were together seemingly the precursors of both the Christian heaven and the Muslim paradise.

The underworld of the Greeks combined these three regions, allowing its judges to separate the good and the bad, and to reward or punish them. According to the poet Hesiod, who flourished in the ninth century BC, the main part of the underworld was Tartarus, a vast area surrounded by a bronze wall and by an encircling triple layer of the darkest night, wherein the gigantic Titans, who were banished there for trying to overthrow the gods, were perpetually imprisoned. Night and her twin sons Sleep and Death also resided there, as did Hades, the god of death, and his wife Persephone, the latter couple living together in a magnificent mansion or palace. The name of Hades (which probably means 'the unseen') was eponymously applied to the whole region. To the west of Tartarus ran a wide river, the Styx, across which dead souls were rowed by the elderly, bearded and unkempt ferryman Charon, always providing, that is, that they brought with them an obolus, a coin with the value of one old penny (which was hopefully placed under the tongue of their corpse) to pay for their passage. Entrance into Tartarus (or Hades) was via a gate guarded by a gigantic three-headed dog named Cerberus, which permitted entry to the wraiths of the dead (but not living adventurers) but devoured any who tried to escape. The Roman poet Virgil (70-19 BC), in his epic the *Aeneid*, says the neck of Cerberus was encircled by writhing snakes.

Hecataeus, the 'father of geography', who lived at Miletus in about 520 BC, described the earth as being disc-shaped, which naturally accounted for the circular shadow seen on the moon during a lunar eclipse. Its land surface, he said, consisted of the northern continent of Europe, which was separated from the southern continent of Asia, made up of north Africa and the Arabian peninsula, by the Mediterranean

Sea, the Black Sea and the Caspian Sea. Around both continents flowed the Ocean Stream, which marked the outer
border of the world, although where the water that flowed off
its edge went was unknown. The centre or 'navel' of this
world disc was said to be the Greek town of Delphi, where
the god Apollo had his temple and oracle.

The realm of Hades, which lay beneath the disc, could be
reached via certain surface apertures, the most important of
which stood in a grove of black poplars somewhere on the
north shore of the Ocean Stream, into which flowed the
conjoined waters of the rivers Phlegethon (or 'fiery') and
Cocytus (or 'lamentation'), both tributaries of the Styx.
Homer tells us that the wily Odysseus made the long journey
there by boat in order to consult the dead seer Teiresias,
whom he was able to lure to the surface, along with many
other famous wraiths, by making certain sacrifices and liba-
tions, although his success in this regard says little for the ability of the wall around Hades to keep them in. Other
cavernous entrances to the underworld, such as that at
Taenarus in Laconica (from which black smoke constantly
emerged) and Aornum in Thesprotia were more accessibly
situated. The name Aornum, or Aornos, means 'a place without birds' and indicates that the noxious fumes coming from
the cave were fatal to bird life. Similar portals were also
provided by volcanic vents and sulphurous springs elsewhere.

The distance of Tartarus beneath us is also given by Hesiod,
who in the *Theogony* tells us:

> An anvil made of bronze, falling from heaven,
> Would fall nine nights and days, and on the tenth
> Would reach the earth, and if the anvil fell
> From earth, would fall again nine nights and days
> And come to Tartarus upon the tenth.

Thus heaven or the sky, according to the poet, is the same height
above the earth as Tartarus is beneath it. But he obviously had no
idea how far an anvil would fall in nine nights and days, which is

simply a poetic way of saying 'a very long way'. Indeed, if we
assume for a moment that Tartarus really does lie beneath us, the
distance suggested by Hesiod is a preposterous overestimate. We
now know that an object falls under the influence of gravity at
the accelerating velocity of 32.2 feet (or 9.8 metres) per second
per second, which enables us to determine, by using the formula

$time = \frac{\pi}{2\theta}$ (where π = 3.142 and $\theta = \sqrt{\frac{g}{R}}$, while g = gravi-
tational acceleration and R = the Earth's radius),

that if an anvil was dropped down a vertical, airless tube the
3963.5 miles (equatorial radius) to the Earth's centre, the deepest
possible point, it would reach its destination in only 21 minutes.

The Greeks thought that when people died their wraiths
wandered around in the vicinity of their corpses until the god
Hermes (the Roman Mercury) arrived to take them down to
the underworld. Hermes was therefore the first divine being
encountered after death, and his comforting presence and
additional function as a guide accords with the experience of
many modern people revived from apparent death, who have
often reported finding themselves, while unconscious and yet
out of their bodies, in the presence of a similar spiritual escort.

As Hermes had no assistants, he was of necessity required
to marshal a crowd of wraiths before conducting them
together into a suitable opening in the earth. They then journeyed downwards until they came to the river Styx, where the
god passed them on to Charon, the ferryman, who would,
upon receiving the aforementioned obolus, row them across
to Hades' realm. Wraiths without the requisite cash were
condemned to remain forever on that dismal shore, which
naturally made death a daunting experience for penniless
beggars who only had penniless beggars for friends. The
wraiths of unburied corpses were also refused passage. As
both the Greeks and the Romans never cremated or interred
their dead before seven days had passed, this meant that every
wraith had to loiter for at least that long on the bank of the
Styx, although some, such as those lost at sea who would not
have an obolus either, would probably always remain there.

Although the geography of Hades' realm underwent certain poetic modifications over the years, it was later thought to consist of three distinct regions, named the Asphodel Fields, the Elysian Fields, and Tartarus proper. All wraiths arriving at the *pylades* or gate of Hades were first sniffily inspected by Cerberus, its fierce three-headed canine guardian, which could apparently distinguish real wraiths from visiting doubles, and then went through it into the Asphodel Fields. This was a rather flat, gloomy expanse of open country, wherein grew, as its name indicates, extensive stands of asphodel, the earthly version of which (*Asphodeline lutea*) is a 3-foot tall white- or yellow-flowered plant of the lily family, which grows on rather poor rocky soils throughout Greece. The wraiths remained in the Asphodel Fields until individually summoned to appear before one or other of the three underworld judges, named Minos, Aecus and Rhadamanthus, who evaluated the quality of the lives they had led. Wraiths from the continent of Europe were judged by Aecus, those from Asia by Rhadamanthus, while Minos served as the final arbiter of all difficult cases. Their verdict determined to which of the three underworld regions each wraith was sent.

From the place of judgement led three roads, one back to the Asphodel Fields, one to the Elysian Fields, and one to Tartarus. Those who had led good and blameless lives were dispatched to Elysium, those who had been wicked or impious were sent to Tartarus, while those who had done nothing to distinguish themselves in either way were returned to the Asphodel Fields, where they would remain to wander aimlessly around in its depressing landscape.

The wraiths that attained passage to the Elysian Fields found themselves in a beautiful country consisting of broad green meadows, delightful gardens and pleasant orchards, watered by streams of clear, pure water, where birds sang gaily, lions gambolled with lambs, and soft breezes blew, while overhead the region's own sun (and moon and stars at night!) shone from an azure sky. This was for the Greeks their heaven in the underworld, and the wraiths that lived there were entirely free to enjoy themselves doing those things which had particularly pleased them in life. Their food was provided by the gardens and orchards, and all that was eaten in one day spontaneously renewed itself for the next. And as there was no work, stress, sickness, ageing, worry or conflict, the conditions in Elysium were broadly similar, when taken together, to those met with by Gilgamesh in the garden of the sun and in Dilmun. Indeed, they are also very like those found by some recent visitors to the next world who have been taken to what they believe is heaven. Furthermore, we must note that by Classical times the Elysian Fields were held by many, like Socrates for example, to lie above ground on real islands in the far west, possibly off the coast of Africa, where in fact are situated the Azores and, further south, Madeira and the Canary Islands, which were alternatively known as the Fortunate Islands or the Isles of the Blessed. In this regard they occupy the place suggested for Dilmun.

However, the wraiths that went to Tartarus had a very different environment with which to contend. Not only was it dark and forbidding, but it was surrounded by a high bronze wall, which itself was circled by the fiery waters of the river Phlegethon. No escape was possible, and the company within consisted entirely of murderers, despots, torturers, blasphemers, adulterers, traitors and the like, who not only breathed in its pervading air of hopelessness, but who were punished for their crimes in various bizarre ways, the worst of which were meted out to those who had offended the gods.

It was there that Sisyphus, for example, who had, among other crimes, betrayed Zeus's abduction of Aegina to her father, was condemned to push a heavy rock to the top of a hill, but which always, just before he reached the summit, slipped from his grasp and rolled down to the bottom, whereupon he had to start all over again; the giant Tityus, whose attempt to rape the goddess Leto had resulted in his being stretched face up on the ground with two vultures pecking endlessly at his liver (which constantly renewed itself); and forty-nine of the fifty daughters of Danaus, known as the Danaids, who were forced to carry water in sieves for having murdered their husbands on their joint wedding nights.

The most relevant of these felons to us is Sisyphus. He was the historical founder (in about 1388 BC) and first king of Ephyre, later renamed Corinth, in the northern Peloponnese, close by the famous isthmus, who gained notoriety by robbing and murdering any travellers that visited the town. Indeed, his ugly habit of doing this by piling huge heaps of rocks on them probably suggested the punishment he eventually received. Sisyphus, however, is said to have died twice. The first time followed his betrayal of Zeus, who angrily ordered Hades himself to carry the monarch to Tartarus. Yet strangely, despite such a direct order, Sisyphus kept Hades waiting for several days before he died, and he later came back to life.

This is the mythological way of saying that Sisyphus in all probability contracted a serious illness, one that often gave rise to a death-like comatose state. That this could be mistaken for the real thing is shown by Sisyphus's warning to his wife not to bury him too quickly if he appeared to die. Moreover, because Hades was reputedly kept waiting by his bedside for about a week, the sickness evidently caused the king to slip in and out of consciousness.

But at last Sisyphus apparently did die, whereupon his wraith separated from his body and journeyed to Hades' realm. He then made his way, or so the myth says, to Persephone, and told her that, as his corpse was unburied, he had no right to be there. He next managed to convince the goddess that, if she allowed him to return to his body for three days, he would make his own funeral arrangements. He promised to return then and undergo the normal underworld judicial procedures. Persephone granted his request, but Sisyphus broke his promise and stayed alive, which can only mean that he recovered consciousness and went on to make a full recovery. Thus Sisyphus's visit to the underworld, when stripped of its mythological elements – but particularly in view of the fact that he is represented as having crossed the Styx before burial and without an obolus – is clearly a genuine NDE, one of the earliest on record.

Other features of the Sisyphus story indicate that the area around Ephyre at the time of its founding was marshy: the town, for example, had a perpetual spring named Peirene, which means 'of the osiers', whilst its first inhabitants reputedly sprang from mushrooms. Osiers, a type of willow, and mushrooms are both associated with damp, marshy places, which would have resulted in malaria (a disease still common in Greece – Lord Byron was a famous victim in 1811) and various water-born infections being endemic to the area. Hence Sisyphus probably fell victim of one or other of these.

Another early NDE was undergone by Alcestis, the beautiful wife of Admetus, king of Pherae in Thessaly. The myth relates that Admetus contracted a serious ailment. He consulted an oracle to learn what his chances were of surviving it, but was told that, having reached his fated time to die, he would only recover if someone close to him voluntarily died in his place. When neither of his elderly parents were prepared to sacrifice themselves in this way, the devoted Alcestis attempted to kill herself by drinking poison, but while the dose put her into a death-like coma, it proved insufficient to complete the job. According to the myth, when Alcestis reached the underworld, Persephone (whose traumatic abduction by Hades had evidently turned into something of a feminist) was horrified to discover that she had committed suicide merely to save a husband, and sent her back to her body. This implies of course that Alcestis recovered from the effects of the poison, whereas Admetus, despite his wife's best and most noble effort, shortly thereafter died.

Furthermore, because the near death of both Sisyphus and Alcestis brought them into the presence of Persephone, whose residence in Hades only lasted for four months each year (the Greek winter), it appears that Sisyphus and Admetus went down with their infections in that season, when mortality rates are generally higher, which helps explain their anxiety about their chances of recovery.

The Greek myths also include several instances of living men who supposedly journeyed to the underworld, the most famous of whom was Orpheus. His story is fascinating because it shows how what was probably a temporary recovery from clinical death became in the course of time a mythological volte-face.

It is said that when Orpheus, the most talented singer and musician of antiquity, returned with Jason and the other Argonauts from Colchis, where they had sailed to recover the Golden Fleece, he fell in love with and married the beautiful Eurydice. But unhappily, not long afterwards Eurydice fell victim to the lustful attention of one Aristeaus, and while being chased by the would-be rapist, stepped on a venomous snake and died from its bite.

The grief-stricken Orpheus resolved to rescue her from the underworld and, carrying his lyre with him, he entered the cavern at Aornum and made his own way down to the Styx. He then musically charmed Charon into rowing him across the river, likewise sang the fierce Cerberus to sleep, and soon reached the palace of Hades. The god of death was similarly susceptible to his singing and he agreed to release Eurydice back to the upper world, on condition that Orpheus did not look at her before they reached the sunlight. Unhappily, the anxious Orpheus turned to see if she was still following him when he reached the cavernous exit to the underworld, and thus lost her for ever.

In evaluating this myth, we cannot help noticing that Eurydice's death by snake bite is essentially the same as that of Alcestis, who drank poison. And while everyone else who went to Hades' realm required a guide to lead them there, Orpheus did not, which in itself suggests that he did not journey underground himself.

Moreover, while a wraith certainly does return to its physical self if the latter is resuscitated (as indeed happened with both Sisyphus and Alcestis), it would have been pointless to bring back Eurydice's wraith from the next realm (by whatever means) if her body was really dead, as she would not have been able to enter and reanimate it again. Hence I suspect that what really happened is that Eurydice was bitten by a snake and clinically died, that she was lamented over and possibly even sung to by the grieving Orpheus (which may have happened in a cave), that she briefly recovered – perhaps to the extent of opening her eyes or taking a breath – but that he picked her up too hastily in his overjoyed state and carried her outside, and the sudden movement resulted in her irreversible death. If so, the essence of the myth is all there: the familiar playing and singing of Orpheus which helped return Eurydice to consciousness, thereby 'winning over' Charon, Cerberus and Hades; the wraith of Eurydice briefly returning to her body from the underworld, but being prevented from staying longer by Orpheus doing what he should not have done – moving her too precipitately.

There is one adventurer into the underworld whose story is worth considering in more detail, as it contains elements that are relevant to our study. The man in question is Heracles (the Roman Hercules), the greatest but also the most psychologically flawed of the Greek heroes.

Enormously strong and with bisexual tendencies, Heracles strangely allowed himself to be treated like a slave by both Eurystheus, king of Mycenae and Argos, whose lover he also reputedly became, and Omphale, queen of Lydia, with whom he fell in love and whom he married. He also enjoyed wearing her clothes, thereby revealing a transvestite propensity. He additionally fathered numerous bastards on different women, killed often and generally without remorse, and suffered at least one period of madness, when his perceptions and grip on reality became so distorted that he murdered six of his own children and two nephews. Today, he would probably be diagnosed as a dangerous psychopath, and would no doubt be confined to a very secure mental hospital.

From about the age of eighteen, Heracles wore a lion's pelt and used a large club as his preferred weapon, more suited to a denizen of the Stone Age than the late Bronze Age in which he lived. Yet he was well educated, having been taught lyre playing, literature, mathematics, philosophy, and the use of different weapons by his various tutors. He was thus an odd combination of the archaic and the modern (in Bronze Age terms), or the wild and the civilized. In this regard he mirrored the different personalities of Gilgamesh and Enkidu, especially as Gilgamesh had once shown a similar preoccupation with sex and with the killing of lions.

Heracles is best known for performing the Twelve Labours, a set of difficult tasks imposed on him by Eurystheus, to whom the hero offered his services on the advice of an oracle, in order to make amends for the slaughter of his children. While performing the Labours Heracles also killed several villains, founded cities, unblocked rivers, righted wrongs and generally did good, so gaining heroic status and becoming, as his contemporaries and later Greeks believed, 'the friend of all mankind'.

The Labours included the killing of certain dangerous and destructive beasts, such as a lion, a Hydra and some large birds, and capturing others; cleaning out a dung-filled cattle yard; and stealing the girdle of an Amazon queen. The last two, however, were altogether different from the rest and were in fact added by Eurystheus to what were originally Ten Labours, when the king decided that two of these did not count – Heracles had received help in killing the Lernaean Hydra, the Second Labour, and a payment in cattle for cleaning out the Augeian stables, the Fifth Labour. Hence in this respect alone they stand apart, which in turn suggests that there is more to them than meets the eye.

The Eleventh Labour required Heracles to journey to the garden of the Hesperides, sited on the slopes of Mount Atlas, and from it bring back the golden apples. As the garden was situated where the sun was believed to set, Heracles's journey is reminiscent of the one made by Gilgamesh, who travelled west to seek the secret of eternal life from Utnapishtim. And just as Heracles seems to combine the traits displayed by Gilgamesh and Enkidu, the garden of the Hesperides is likewise a combination of the garden of the setting sun on the far side of Mount Mashu and Dilmun. Indeed, some scholars think this means that the Eleventh Labour is merely a retelling of Gilgamesh's adventure using Heracles as the protagonist, particularly as apples are tr ditionally associated with longevity – as the saying 'An apple a day keeps the doctor away' indicates. But apples were also believed to impart wisdom, which implies, along with the fact that the tree on which they grow (which does not feature in the Mesopotamian story) was guarded by a serpent, that its source could equally well have been the Hebrew Garden of Eden.

However, there are elements in the tale of the Eleventh Labour which suggest that it has a deeper meaning and an independent origin. First, there were three Hesperides, the daughters of Atlas, the giant who stood on top of the mountain holding aloft the sky. Their number gives them an immediate connection with the underworld and thus with death, for as we have seen, the Greeks closely associated three with both, which arose because Hades, the god of death, was the third and last son born to his father Cronus. Moreover, because Atlas was a personification of the mountain itself, his daughters must therefore have arisen from the earth of that holy spot, indicating that they were really wraiths from the underworld, like those tempted to the surface by Odysseus.

The myth also relates that, when Heracles set out to find the Hesperidean garden, he did not know where to look, which implies that Eurystheus did not either. If so, this surely means that the king had only heard rumours or stories about a divine garden whose attainment brought an otherwise unobtainable wisdom to the finder. To discover its location, Heracles was therefore obliged to waken, at the behest of some river-nymphs, a sleeping and elderly sea-god named Nereus, whose protean changes of form made it difficult at first for the hero to hold on to him. He eventually succeeded in doing so and getting him to talk. Indeed, both the river-nymphs and the sleeping sea-god symbolize the fact that the quest can be fulfilled during sleep or unconsciousness (crossing a river, stream or sea is sometimes used as a metaphor for travel to another realm when dreaming), just as Enkidu went down to the underworld while asleep. Heracles' struggle with Nereus, however, shows that it is none the less very hard to accomplish.

Indeed, the difficulty was such that Nereus is represented as advising Heracles to get Atlas to enter the garden and steal the apples for him. This Atlas did once Heracles had shot and killed the guardian serpent with an arrow and temporarily relieved him of his burden of the sky. As the name Atlas means 'he who dares', this is a mythological way of saying that Heracles overcame his doubts and fears (which must have been considerable, given the uniqueness and the momentous nature of the task), and entered a sacred cave on a holy mountain (we do not need to assume he actually went to Mount Atlas), where he either fell into a deep sleep or, more probably, into a drug-induced trance (serpents or snakes have long been associated with the taking of hallucinatory drugs). This enabled him to dream a divine dream – in other words, to separate his conscious double from his body – and travel to the Hesperidean or heavenly garden, whereby he achieved knowledge of the next dimension of being that is normally only experienced by those who die or have an NDE. Furthermore, because the region around Mycenae was an ideal habitat for mushrooms (as is suggested by its name, which derives from *mycos*, meaning 'fungus' – hence mycology), it is likely that they were the source of the drug which Heracles may have eaten.

After Heracles had delivered the 'golden apples' of knowledge to Eurystheus, he was given his final task, the Twelfth Labour, which required him to descend into the underworld and bring back the three-headed dog Cerberus. Although this was an impossible mission for a living man, Heracles evidently had no qualms about undertaking it, presumably because, having learned how to separate his double from his sleeping body and reach the garden of the Hesperides, he suspected that Hades' realm could be entered in a similar way.

Revealingly, he first travelled to the town of Eleusis, near Athens, famous for being the place where Demeter stayed during her search for her abducted daughter Kore, and where an important religious festival in their joint honour named the Mysteries took place. Owing to an oath of secrecy which all participants in the Mysteries oı Eleusis took, we still do not know what they entailed, although some very profound and life-changing experiences did take place, which involved not only marvellous sights and sounds, but inner revelations into what was surely the true nature and meaning of both life and death – Demeter representing life, and her daughter Kore, who became Persephone each winter, death.

Because at that time only residents of Athens were allowed to participate in the Mysteries, Heracles was initiated into a shorter ceremony specially devised for him, thereafter known as the Lesser Mysteries, dedicated solely to Kore. This suggests that during the ceremony Heracles was told the means by which he could gain access to the underworld, where Kore resided as Persephone. Furthermore, because Heracles is credited with the discovery of two particular plants, namely monkshood (*Aconitum sp.*) and black henbane (*Hyoscyamus niger*), which are both poisonous and contain potent mind-altering substances, it seems that the secret lay with the seeds, leaves and other parts of them, and that the correct mixture and dosage was revealed to him by the priests. If he ate henbane (so called because it is deadly to hens), which is also known as 'insane root', it might explain the type of madness that afflicted him, causing him to mistake his sons and nephews for enemies and kill them, for the active substances hyoscyamine and hyoscine grossly distort the perceptions. This accords with the opinion of some early mythographers, who say that Heracles' madness only happened after he had performed the Twelfth Labour.

Heracles descended into the underworld, according to the mythical account, via either the cavern at Taenarus or a similar orifice in the earth, which must therefore have been the place where he took the drugs and entered a divine trance.

JOURNEYS TO HEAVEN AND TO HELL

Hermes and Athene reportedly guided him downwards, although the latter, being the goddess of wisdom and one of the Olympians, would never ordinarily enter Hades' realm, so that her presence must symbolize the fact that the true nature of his journey was not to bring back a dog, but to obtain knowledge about the darker parts of the next world.

Hence it seems that Heracles, while in a trance, or more probably, if we recall that both aconite and henbane are poisonous, clinically dead, became separated from his body in his wraith form. He was then met by a guide, identified as Hermes, who led him to the edge of a broad river, which many others have seen, and which he believed was the Styx. He was rowed across the river by the ferryman Charon.

On the other bank Heracles met the wraiths of a former hero named Meleager, whose sister he promised to marry, and the Gorgon Medusa, whose petrifying glance was fortunately no longer potent, although why they were wandering around unaccompanied is not explained. He also came across and released Theseus, but not his companion Peirithous, from the seat in which he was held. The pair had both descended into Tartarus four years before, which suggests either that Heracles may once have revived Theseus from clinical death or that he brought this about, while in the next world, by encouraging his wraith to return to his body. He was evidently unable to help Peirithous in the same manner. Either way, this will certainly have happened four hours or four days after Theseus died, not four years.

After releasing a wraith from under a block of stone and wrestling with Menoetius, Hades' cattleman, one of whose beeves he wished to sacrifice, the hero came into the presence of Persephone and Hades, the former greeting him warmly. Their meeting was brief, but Heracles gained permission from Hades to carry Cerberus back to the upper world, on condition that he did not harm the hound by using his bow and arrows or his club. Heracles thereupon grabbed Cerberus around the throat, choked him into submission, and carried him, with assistance from Athene, although still with considerable difficulty, back across the Styx and up to the surface.

The meeting between Heracles and Hades and Persephone suggests of course that he clinically died, that his separated wraith was conducted by a guide to the boundary of the dark realm where he encountered some other wraiths, and that he had considerable difficulty in waking from his death-like state, which is symbolized by his struggle in carrying the three-headed death-hound up to the surface. Together, these suggest that Heracles' journey to the underworld did occur, although it was not made by the living hero, which is impossible, but by his wraith.

These seemingly wholly mythological stories – the quest of Gilgamesh, the last two Labours of Heracles and the three apparently nonsensical visits made by Enkidu, Sisyphus and Alcestis to the underworld – are all therefore revealed as early double or wraith separation experiences. Two of the protagonists went to paradisial gardens, and four to the dark realm of death. We must note that the gardens were situated on the western border of our world, which gave them light, whereas the nether world, as then conceived, lay underground and was forbiddingly dark. Three of the separations, those of Enkidu, Gilgamesh and Heracles' first, occurred during sleep or a trance, the other three during a state of clinical death, one of which (Sisyphus) happened during sickness, one during a suicide attempt (Alcestis), and one (Heracles' second) following the ingestion of dangerous drugs designed to bring it about.

3

From Hades to Heaven

For thou hast authority over life and death,
And thou leadest down to the gates of Hades,
   and leadest up again.
But though a man may slay by his wickedness,
Yet the spirit that is gone forth he turneth not again,
Neither giveth release to the soul that Hades hath received.
                              From *The Wisdom of Solomon*

Heracles is significant not only for his NDE which allowed him to visit Hades, but also because at his death he was said to have been taken up to heaven. His ascension made it possible for the pagan Greeks to believe that other benefactors of mankind, like Asclepius, the 'father of medicine', had been similarly blessed. This in turn encouraged the supposition, notably among those Greeks who later converted to Christianity, that the wraiths of good people were likewise rewarded by being carried aloft to live in a beautiful, light-filled garden called heaven.

As we have noted, the sky and the summits of mountains were regarded in early pagan times as divine and thus both inaccessible and off-limits to ordinary mortals. One could travel to them only if a particular deity so willed it and that deity would of course provide the necessary transportation. Thus Ganymedes, for example, the son of King Tros of Troy and the handsomest youth alive, was reputedly abducted by Zeus in the form of an eagle and carried up to the summit of Mount Olympus, where he became Zeus's catamite and the cup bearer to the other gods. But while Ganymedes was granted immortality, he was taken aloft while still alive, so that the divine gift he received was for the shameful desire he inflamed and the use to which he was put, rather than being a post-mortem reward for a life well spent. Another mortal who was likewise taken to the summit of Mount Olympus, although as an invited dinner guest, was Tantalus, whose story is related in the next chapter.

It was the divine paternity of Heracles, along with the greatness of his life, that made him a suitable candidate for apotheosis. This came about through the strange circumstances of his death. Heracles had kept his promise to Meleager by marrying his sister Deianeira, but then broke her heart with his continual infidelities. She tried to win back his love by anointing a shirt with the blood and semen of the centaur Nessus, who had been killed by Heracles when he tried to rape her. The dying centaur had told Deianeira that if Heracles was given the impregnated shirt to wear, she would never again have cause to worry about him running after other women.

However, the shirt of Nessus did not act as a love-philtre, as she had hoped. It instead burned into Heracles's skin and flesh, causing him excruciating pain, while at the same time resisting all his efforts to tear it from his body. In his agony, the hero hurriedly constructed a funeral pyre for himself on the summit of Mount Oeta, intending to die in its flames. But after he had laid himself on the pyre and it had been ignited by a passing shepherd, Zeus obliterated it with a thunderbolt and then bore the divine portion of Heracles up to Mount Olympus, where he was welcomed into the company of the gods.

Having been taken to heaven, Heracles was said to have married Hebe, the daughter of Hera, and to have been given the role of porter to the gates of Olympus, opening and closing them for any god and goddess who had business on earth. His elevation entitled him to divine worship, and indeed numerous shrines and temples dedicated to him were erected throughout the pagan world. Yet despite becoming a god, Heracles was not admitted into the sacred company of the twelve Olympians, which could only have come about if one of them had vacated his or her place for him (as Hestia did for Dionysus). This explains why, although he was admitted to heaven, he had to be content with the relatively lowly position of gatekeeper.

The other odd fact about Heracles' death is that whereas the divine part of him was deified, his wraith, like that of all mortals, went to Hades, where it was briefly brought to the surface by Odysseus, when he journeyed to the northern entrance of the dark realm to consult with the dead seer Teiresias. 'His looks,' noted Homer, 'were as sombre as the blackest night, and with his naked bow in hand and an arrow on the string he glanced ferociously this way and that as though at any moment he might shoot.' It was on this occasion that Odysseus also spoke with the wraith of Achilles, who famously remarked of his residence in the land of the dead, 'Put me on earth again, and I would rather be a serf in the house of some landless man, with little enough for himself to live on, than king of all these dead men that have done with life.'

The Greek philosopher Plato (427-347 BC), like his mentor Socrates and indeed most of his countrymen, believed that the wraith or soul survives the death of the physical body, and that in the next world it is held accountable for any misdeeds the person has done while alive. Yet neither philosopher considered the conventional Greek belief in an underworld to which everyone went to be accurate, which is why, at the end of his masterwork *The Republic*, Plato has Socrates recount the post-mortem experience of a man named Er, who was killed in a battle and who not only came back from the dead but remembered what he had seen on 'the other side'. Er's recollections are important because he claimed that there exists, somewhere high above the earth's surface, a place reserved for the good, and which is therefore a separate celestial heaven.

Although the short section about Er in *The Republic* is usually entitled 'The Myth of Er', the use of the word 'myth' does not mean that it is untrue or fictitious, but rather that Er's experience was so unique and personal that it could be neither validated nor dismissed by philosophic reasoning. It was, in other words, reported but unproven. But the fact that Er's account is similar to those of others who have returned to life, suggests that Socrates' description of what happened to him is accurate, even though it may have been added to by Plato, who wished to make the philosophical point that the evil of life arises from the pursuit of wealth, power and sensual pleasure.

Socrates says that Er, the son of Armenius and 'a brave man', was a native of the province of Pamphylia, situated in what is now southern Turkey. His place of origin adds credence to the story, for Pamphylia was a relatively little-known backwater in which to set it if it was fictitious. Following his death (fighting against whom we are not told), Er lay unconscious on the battlefield for ten days, surrounded by decaying corpses, until his body was at last collected up and prepared for cremation. A pyre was built by his grieving relatives, and on the twelfth day after the battle he was laid upon it. But then, just as the pyre was about to be lit, and to the absolute astonishment of those gathered around, Er recovered his senses and sat up. He had, quite literally, come back from the dead.

Such an occurrence, while seemingly unlikely, is by no means unprecedented, and indeed I have mentioned several similar instances of recovery in *Buried Alive*, although not all who have returned to life on their funeral pyres have been lucky enough to avoid being burned alive.

But if Er's friends and relatives were astounded by his unexpected revival, they were even more amazed by his account of what happened to him when he was dead:

He said that when his soul left his body it travelled in company with many others till they came to a wonderfully strange place, where

58

there were, close to each other, two gaping chasms in the earth, and opposite and above them two gaping chasms in the sky. Between the chasms sat Judges, who, having delivered their judgement, ordered the just to take the right-hand road that led up through the sky . . . while they ordered the unjust . . . to take the left-hand road that led downwards.

The 'wonderfully strange place' where the judgement occurred was in fact a broad, sunlit meadow, which must have stretched away into the distance, as Er said that when souls returned there from either the sky or the underworld, they next undertook a journey lasting several days to reach the place from which they were whisked off to be reborn. Er also came before the judges, but he was told that, unlike everyone else, he was only there temporarily and had therefore to take a careful note of all that happened, in order to report on what he had seen when he returned to life. This requirement to act as an observer has also been a feature of the NDEs of others.

Er soon noted that while the wraiths of the just ascended into the sky and those of the unjust descended to the underworld, other wraiths were also emerging from the two remaining chasms. They were, he discovered, returning from the sky and from the underworld in order to be reborn. Both types of returnees were glad to meet old friends and comrades again and to discuss their different experiences.

The wraiths who came back from the sky 'told of the delights of heaven and of the wonderful beauty of what they had seen', while those returning from the underworld spoke of the sadness and suffering they had both seen and endured. Er learned that each criminal act or wrongdoing brought a ten-fold penalty, and he described 'the even greater penalties and rewards of those who had honoured or dishonoured the gods or parents or committed murder'. He heard one wraith ask about a fellow Pamphylian named Ardiaeus the Great, who had been a tyrant and murderer 1,000 years earlier. The man was informed that he was still imprisoned in the underworld. The informant added that Ardiaeus, along with some other tyrants, had recently been caught trying to escape via the underworld exit chasm, but this opening had uttered a warning bellow as they approached it, whereupon some fierce-looking guards had taken hold of them, bound them tightly, thrown them down on the roadside and flayed them, then pierced them with sharp thorns and afterwards flung them all into Tartarus. This revealed to Er that no mercy was given in death to those who had been unmerciful in life.

The returned wraiths remained in the meadow for seven days, after which they took an excursion to see the shaft of clear light that apparently ran through the axis of the earth, and to which was attached, at each end, the spindle of Necessity. Nearby sat the three Fates, Necessity's daughters, Lachesis, Clotho and Atropos. A guide called the Interpreter then collected various numbered lots and types of life from the lap of Lachesis, the first of which he tossed amongst the wraiths, each of whom picked up the one that landed beside him or her.

The Interpreter then sprinkled the different types of life on the ground, some of which were human and some animal, and each wraith then selected one from the several variations which matched the number of his or her lot, with many opting to become animals or birds. Thus everyone was given some choice in the life they led after rebirth, which meant that fate (in the guise of Lachesis) was by no means entirely to blame for the misery most people suffered, particularly as 'for the most part they followed the habits of their former life'.

Next, each wraith was appointed its own *daimonion* or guardian angel 'to guide it through life and fulfil its choice', following which they were led by their guardians through a parched desert to the river Lethe (or 'forgetfulness'), from which they were all, with the exception of Er, required to drink. They afterwards fell into a deep sleep on the riverbank, whereupon at midnight they were all suddenly swept up like meteors to be reborn, although Er came to himself lying on a cremation pyre.

The first thing to note in Er's experience is that the

departed wraiths or souls he encountered were exact replicas of their physical selves (as he was himself) and that they had the same sort of awareness and comprehension of their surroundings as before, even to the extent of feeling pleasure and pain. Thus existence in the next world is apprehended by sight, hearing, touch, smell and taste, and everyone there is subject to the same restraints and limitations they endured in life. And while Er went only to the place of judgement, which was a broad meadow somewhat similar to the Asphodel Fields of popular belief but with better illumination, such a 'green field' landscape has frequently been mentioned by those who have made a similar excursion into the afterlife. As this meadow did not exist in the underworld but somewhere seemingly midway between the nether world and heaven, its location may have been on the earth's surface, much like those distant western gardens visited by Gilgamesh and Heracles.

The belief in rebirth or reincarnation, whereby a wraith returns to earth to take up residence in a new human body, probably originated in Egypt or in Asia Minor. Allied to it is the doctrine of metempsychosis, which maintains that a wraith can also be reborn into the body of an animal (or even into a plant), an option which was granted to those wraiths returning to the meadow of judgement described by Er. According to the Greek historian Herodotus, metempsychosis was an Egyptian concept:

[The Egyptians] were also the first people to put forward the doctrine of the immortality of the soul, and to maintain that after death it enters another creature at the moment of that creature's birth. It then makes the round of all living things – animals, birds, and fish – until finally it passes once again, at birth, into the body of a man. The whole period of transmigration occupies three thousand years.

Neither Hesiod nor Homer, our two earliest Greek literary sources, mentions the possibility of rebirth, which implies that the concept was unknown in Greece in the ninth and eighth centuries BC, when they respectively wrote. Tradition in fact ascribes its introduction to Pythagoras, a mathematician and philosopher of the sixth century BC, who is best known today for his famous theorem which states that the square on the hypotenuse of a right-angled triangle is equal to the sum of the squares on the other two sides.

Pythagoras, the gifted son of a distinguished father Mnesarchus, was born on the island of Samos in about 582 BC. His intellectual abilities were matched by his physical prowess, and he not only excelled at music, poetry, mathematics and astronomy but won the olive crown for wrestling at the Olympic Games when he was eighteen years old. He afterwards travelled to Egypt and to Chaldea to complete his education, and learned much from the priests and other wise men of those countries, including their belief in the immortality of the soul and in its reincarnation – although one Greek source says he was taught such things by a priestess at Delphi. Upon settling in Crotona, a Greek colony in southern Italy, where he founded a school of philosophy, he made these notions a central part of his teachings. He died in 497 BC.

Pythagoras claimed to be able to remember all his previous lives. The first of these, he said, was as Aethalides of Thessaly in north-eastern Greece, who was reputedly the son of the god Hermes and the mortal Eupolemeia. Following in his divine father's footsteps, Aethalides eventually became the herald aboard the *Argo*. When he was a youth, Hermes promised him one gift of his choice, with the exception of immortality, and Aethalides opted for the ability to remember all his experiences in life and in death, which explains Pythagoras's unusual recollection of his former incarnations.

In his next existence he was a Dardanian spearman named Euphorbus, who fought at the siege of Troy and who was notable for having inflicted the first wound on Patroclus, the bosom friend of Achilles. Homer recorded that Euphorbus was killed shortly afterwards by Menelaus, who stripped his body of its arms and armour, and who later, on his return to Greece, dedicated his shield to Apollo at his temple at

Didyme (or Branchidae) or, as some say, to Hera at her temple at Mycenae.

He afterwards lived as Hermotimus of Clazomenæ, a city in Ionia (now Vourla in western Turkey). Hermotimus is famous for having been able, upon falling into a deep trance, to leave his body and roam about the world in his double form, which enabled him to report on distant events that he otherwise could have known nothing about. Like Euphorbus before him, Hermotimus recalled his previous lives, and it is said that when he visited the temple where the decaying leather and ivory shield of Euphorbus was hung up among others on public display, he correctly picked it out, despite seeing it for the first time as Hermotimus!

In the next life, the soul or double of Hermotimus and his reincarnatory forebears became a humble fisherman named Pyrrhus, who lived on the island of Delos in the Aegean. He, too, could remember his previous lives. When he died he was reborn on the much larger Aegean island of Samos as Pythagoras.

The voyage of the *Argo* to Colchis took place in 1263 BC and Pythagoras was born in 582 BC, which means the soul that eventually became the sage occupied three other bodies (Euphorbus, Hermotimus and Pyrrhus) between those two dates, a period of 681 years. This gives an average of 170 years and three months between each life, although that between Aethalides and Euphorbus was much shorter, probably only forty-nine years, if we assume that Aethalides was killed during the *Argo* expedition and that Euphorbus was twenty years old when the Trojan War began in 1194 BC.

What is particularly interesting from our point of view is that Pythagoras, in addition to his previous lives, could also remember what happened between them, when his wraith went to the underworld. According to the historian Hieronymus of Rhodes, Pythagoras saw there the wraith of the poet Hesiod chained gibbering to a brass pillar, while that of his fellow bard Homer hung from a tree nearby, surrounded by a writhing mass of hissing serpents. Such degrading punishment was imposed for the impious and disgusting things they had written about the gods. The philosopher also remembered witnessing the wraiths of adulterous men being tortured.

These recollections explain why Pythagoras's disciples were believed to possess a book entitled *The Descent into Hades*, which like the Tibetan *Book of the Dead* served as a travel guide to the underworld and which advised the terminally ill, who either read it or to whom it was read, of what lay ahead of them and the various pitfalls of the journey. Although the book itself is lost, certain paragraphs thought to come from it have been found inscribed on gold tablets recovered from tombs at the Greek colony of Thurium (founded in 444 BC) and elsewhere in southern Italy. These were left for the deceased's wraith to read while it loitered near the body before being taken below by Hermes. One such extract, which refers to a crucial stage of the underground journey, warns the wraith not to drink from the spring of Lethe:

In the mansions of Hades, upon the left, a spring will you find, and near it a white cypress standing; this spring you should not approach. But to the right you will come on another, from Memory's lake a fresh flowing water. Before it are watchers: To them you shall say: 'Of Earth and starry Heaven child am I: my race is of the heavens. But this you must know of yourselves. With thirst, I parch, I perish; quick, give me a drink of the water fresh flowing from Memory's lake!' Then they will give you a drink of the spring of the gods, and then you shall reign with the rest of the heroes.

Similar past life memories were claimed by another Greek philosopher, although these were of the broader metempsychosis variety. This sage was Empedocles of Agrigentum in Sicily, who lived during the fifth century BC, and who is famous for having originated the concept that the world and everything in it is built of four basic building blocks or elements, namely earth, water, air and fire, an idea which was accepted almost without challenge for the next 2,000 years. Regarding his previous lives, Empedocles claimed that, 'before now, I was born a boy and a maid, a bush and a bird, and a dumb fish leaping out of the sea', which gave him a very intimate acquaintance with three of his four elements (earth, air and water). He gained the necessary knowledge of fire in 430 BC when he committed suicide by jumping into the flaming volcanic cone of Mount Etna. He hoped that this would end his cycle of lives and ensure that his wraith was taken to the realm of the gods.

The first Roman epic poet Quintus Ennius (239–169 BC), the author of the famous *Annals*, claimed to have once fallen asleep on Mount Helicon in Greece, the home of the Muses, and dreamed that the ghost of Homer appeared to him. The ghost explained the doctrine of metempsychosis to Ennius and added that he had inherited Homer's soul, which had come to him by way of a peacock!

If metempsychosis happens then it is possible, as John Gay (1685–1732) suggests in the following lines from his poem 'Trivia', that those who are cruel to animals may be punished in their next life by becoming one of the poor beasts on whom they inflicted their outrages:

> If, as the Samian taught, the soul revives,
> And, shifting seats, in other bodies lives:
> Severe shall be the brutal coachman's change,
> Doom'd in a hackney horse the town to range!
> Carmen, transform'd, the groaning load shall draw
> Whom other tyrants with the lash shall awe.

But while the concept of reincarnation was widely accepted by pagans and by many early Christians, it was later censured by the Church as heretical, owing to the fact that it contradicted the promised resurrection of the body at Judgement Day. For obviously, if a soul had lived within several human bodies, it could not possibly reinhabit all of them when they are simultaneously raised from the dead. And there was also the troubling possibility, as St Augustine pointed out, that if a mother returned to life as a girl, she might incestuously marry her own son!

To the Greeks, however, such ideas led to the general supposition that reincarnation was a blessing conferred on those who attained the Elysian Fields, and who could, when they chose, opt to enter a new body and live on earth again – although as we have noted, Plato reports Er as saying that even wraiths who were sent to Tartarus were allowed to be reborn once they had been punished for their former sins, which offered some hope to the wicked. Later, it was held that all wraiths who had been reborn three times and who had three times entered Elysium were further rewarded by being taken to the Fortunate Islands or the Isles of the Blessed, which were presumably even more delightful places, where they lived an idyllic existence for the rest of eternity.

Roman tradition likewise held that Romulus, who founded Rome with his twin brother Remus in 743 BC, had returned to heaven following his mysterious and possibly supernatural disappearance in 714. This remarkable fact was reported to his fellow citizens by an aged and highly respected senator named Julius Proculus, who claimed to have met him 'in a form more noble and august than ever, and clad in bright and shining armour' when returning to Rome not long afterwards by road. Moreover, Julius said that not only did Romulus tell him he had returned to the heavenly place whence he had come, which meant that he had come to earth from heaven to live as Romulus and found Rome, but that he was the god Quirinus and would thereafter 'ever be propitious' to the city. Temples were soon erected to the new god, and indeed a festival in his honour called the Quirinalia was celebrated in Rome every March.

Romulus's evident godhead was made more believable to the Roman populace by the associated claim that he and his brother Remus had been fathered on their mortal mother Ilia by the god Mars. Hence Romulus, like Heracles, Asclepius (reputedly the son of Apollo) and indeed Jesus Christ, was of

66

divine ancestry, and like them was born on earth to fulfil a particular mission, which in his case was the founding of Rome.

The next most important step in the acceptance of a celestial residence for the dead was the deification of some of Rome's emperors. This was a major leap of faith, for it allowed pagans to believe in the possibility that entry into heaven could be achieved by mortals like themselves, who had reached the heights on earth and who had contributed to the general good of all. The first man to be deified was Julius Caesar, who held the office of Dictator, and after him Augustus, the first emperor, then Claudius, Vespasian and Titus, among others, all of whom had temples erected to them. Moreover, this belief was seemingly verified by an elderly ex-praetor who had watched the cremation of Augustus, and who reported seeing the wraith of the emperor rising upwards into the sky amid the flames.

The witnessing of wraiths ascending into the sky became quite frequent among pious early Christians, and while sceptics may regard such sightings as visual hallucinations, there is a number of cases on record in which the upwardly moving wraith was seen by someone at a distance who had no idea that the person concerned was dead.

Thus when the Egyptian hermit St Anthony (AD 251–356) was living on Mount Kolzim, near the Red Sea, he one day happened to see the wraith of a man being carried into the sky. Anthony asked God who had died, and a disembodied voice told him it was Ammon, the chief of a group of monks living in the Natron valley, or Wadi-an-Natrun, thirteen days' journey away. And Ammon had indeed passed away at his monastery then.

Likewise, when Pachomius, the abbot of the monastery at Tabenna (founded by him in about AD 320), learned that a monk at the Beth Raya monastery was sick and dying and wished to be blessed by him, he immediately set out to perform that duty, accompanied by some fellow monks. But 2 miles from Beth Raya, Pachomius was stopped by the sound of a voice from the sky. Looking up, he saw the wraith of the monk he was going to bless being carried aloft by hymn-singing angels, although nothing was either heard or seen by those with him. He therefore told them that they were too late, and sent them all back to their own monastery. When they afterwards enquired about the sick monk, they learned that he had departed from the world on the same day and at the same time as Pachomius had seen his vision.

The Jews of Old Testament times, like the ancient Greeks and indeed the Romans, believed that the souls of the dead were taken below ground. They called this subterranean place Sheol. Their heaven was accordingly empty of wraiths and was thought to consist of the following three divisions. The first was the aerial heaven above us where the winds gusted and birds flew; the second was the crystal ceiling above this in which were posited the fixed stars; and lastly, the third heaven was the home of God himself and his attendant angels.

A vision of the third heaven was seen by Jacob when he stopped for the night while travelling between Beersheba and Haran (in about 1700 BC), and laid his head on some stones and went to sleep.

And he dreamed, and behold a ladder set up on the earth, and the top of it reached to heaven: and behold the angels of God ascending and descending on it. And, behold, the Lord stood above it, and said, I *am* the Lord God of Abraham thy father, and the God of Isaac: the land whereon thou liest, to thee I will give it, and to thy seed. (*Genesis*, XXVIII,12–13)

But while the third heaven of the Jews is not a place to which the wraiths of mortals are normally admitted, there is none the less one instance in the Old Testament of a living person being lifted up into the sky and mysteriously vanishing. The man concerned was Elijah of Tish or Thisbe in Gilead, a desert prophet, who was taken aloft in about 896 BC after having crossed the River Jordan with his disciple Elisha.

And it came to pass, as they still went on, and talked, that, behold, *there appeared* a chariot of fire, and horses of fire, and parted them both asunder: and Elijah went up by a whirlwind into heaven. And Elisha saw *it*, and he cried, My father, my father, the chariot of Israel, and the horsemen thereof. And he saw him no more: and he took hold of his own clothes, and rent them in two pieces. He took up also the mantle of Elijah that fell from him, and went back and stood by the bank of Jordan. (*2 Kings*, II, 11–13)

The watching 'sons of the prophets' from Beth-el and Jericho, who had warned Elijah that God would take him away that day, were concerned that 'the Spirit of the Lord hath taken him up, and cast him upon some mountain, or into some valley', which would certainly have occurred if the 'whirlwind' had been a natural phenomenon. They therefore urged Elisha to have the surrounding area searched by a group of fifty men, to which, after initially objecting, he agreed. The assembled search party then spent three days combing the area without finding Elijah's body. So the search was called off, and it was assumed that Elijah had been retained somewhere in the sky.

Elijah's disappearance was as mysterious as that of the patriarch Enoch, the father of Methuselah, who some 2,000 years earlier had vanished without trace, as is briefly described in *Genesis*: 'Enoch walked with God: and he *was* not; for God took him'. This led to the supposition, particularly among Christian writers of the Middle Ages, that the two men continued to exist in some aerial dwelling place midway between earth and the starry second heaven, much as Utnapishtim apparently still lived in the garden beyond 'the waters of death'. Such a notion is encapsulated in Thomas Bulfinch's *Legends of Charlemagne*: 'St John, conducting Astolpho, rejoined his companions. These were the patriarch Enoch and the prophet Elijah; neither of whom had yet seen his dying day, but, taken from our lower world, were dwelling in a region of peace and joy, in a climate of eternal spring, till the last trumpet shall sound.'

The most famous ascension into the air is that of Jesus, who was carried aloft from Mount Olivet forty days after his resurrection. This miraculous happening is only briefly related in the Gospels of St Mark and St Luke, although the latter saint describes it in rather more detail in the *Acts of the Apostles*. Jesus had gone to Mount Olivet accompanied by the apostles and several of his other disciples, to whom he gave some final words of advice and counsel:

And when he had spoken these things, while they beheld, he was taken up; and a cloud received him out of their sight. And while they looked steadfastly toward heaven as he went up, behold, two men stood by them in white apparel; Which also said, Ye men of Galilee, why stand ye gazing up into heaven? this same Jesus, which is taken up from you into heaven, shall so come in like manner as ye have seen him go into heaven. (*Acts*, I, 9–11)

While Jesus was carried up into the sky, or into the first heaven of the Jews, until he disappeared into a cloud, it is evident from what the two angels say that his ultimate destination was the third heaven occupied by God. In this respect his ascension was almost identical to that of Heracles, who like him was the child of a divine father and a mortal mother. Both were carried aloft from a mountain, and although Heracles' exit from the world was more dramatic, with the destruction of his funeral pyre and his mortal self by a thunderbolt, it was their divine component that was taken away, that of Heracles going to reside with his father Zeus and the other gods on the summit of Mount Olympus, while the resurrected Jesus (whose outer appearance was very different from that of his previous physical self) went to the third heaven of God his father.

Jesus was brought up in an orthodox Jewish family and doubtless learned from his teachers that the wraiths of the departed go below ground to Sheol, where the wicked are punished in a separate region known as Gehenna, which is the equivalent of the Greek Tartarus. Indeed, Jesus typically spoke only of heaven – that is, the third heaven – as the abode of God, as in the Lord's Prayer, which begins 'Our Father, which art in heaven, Hallowed be thy name.' Yet he often talked about the kingdom of heaven, which he typically did by way of parables, the most famous being that of the mustard seed:

The kingdom of heaven is like to a grain of mustard seed, which a man took, and sowed in his field: Which indeed is the least of seeds: but when it is grown, it is the greatest among herbs, and becometh a tree, so that the birds of the air come and lodge in the branches thereof. (*Matthew*, XIII, 31–2).

Although the parables of Jesus are beautifully expressed and make use of everyday objects and situations, they do not give the modern reader a clear idea of what he was talking about, although taken together they seem to suggest that the kingdom of heaven is not some other-worldly paradise into which the just and righteous ascend after death but rather an earthly kingdom which will be established following the Day of Judgement and his Second Coming. Indeed, Jesus revealingly said that his father is the God of the living, not the dead, and warned that the Day of Judgement would come suddenly and unexpectedly, which required a constant readiness for its arrival, adding: 'When the Son of Man shall come in his glory, and all the holy angels with him, then shall he sit upon his throne in glory: And before him shall be gathered all nations: and he shall separate them one from another, as a shepherd divideth *his* sheep from the goats.' (*Matthew* XXV, 31–2)

Jesus reportedly raised three people from the dead, namely the daughter of Jairus, the son of the widow of Nain and Lazarus (the brother of Mary and Martha), although unfortunately none of them say anything about their experiences in the next world. Yet Jesus did relate in another of his parables the post-mortem experience of a beggar, coincidentally also named Lazarus, who after death was taken into the bosom of Abraham, whereas the rich man at whose door he had fruitlessly sought charity, went down to Gehenna. The two places are represented as being separated by a great and impassable divide, across which the tormented rich man is none the less able to shout to Abraham.

And he cried and said, Father Abraham, have mercy on me, and send Lazarus, that he may dip the tip of his finger in water, and cool my tongue; for I am tormented in this flame. But Abraham said, Son, remember that thou in thy lifetime receivedst thy good things, and likewise Lazarus evil things: but now he is comforted, and thou art tormented. And beside all this, between us and you there is a great gulf fixed: so that they which would pass from hence to you cannot; neither can they pass to us, that *would come* from thence. (*Luke*, XVI, 24–6).

But where is Abraham? Regarding his death, Genesis says only that 'Abraham gave up the ghost, and died of a good old age, an old man, and full of years; and was gathered to his people', which reveals that he too went underground to Sheol and not to the third heaven.

It is pertinent to note that while Jesus expected to be taken to heaven at his death, he also promised this blessing to one of the two thieves (or, more correctly, bandits) with whom he was crucified. According to St Luke, the man, after commenting that he and his companions were criminals and deserved execution, unlike himself who had done nothing wrong, asked Jesus to remember him when he came into his kingdom. The Lord replied: 'Verily I say unto thee, today shalt thou be with me in paradise.' His use of the word 'paradise' is significant, for it derives from the Old Persian word *pairidaeza*, which means a park or garden, such as were traditionally planted by Middle Eastern monarchs and which were shady and delightful retreats from the surrounding dusty desert. Hence Jesus' promise indicated that during the three days before he rose from the dead, he anticipated finding himself in such a place.

In the years following Jesus' ascension into heaven, his message and teachings were taken to different parts of the

Mediterranean world by the apostles and his other disciples, the most important and influential of whom was Paul of Tarsus. As a young man Paul (or Saul, as he was then known) had taken a leading part in persecuting the followers of Jesus, whom he regarded as yet another false Messiah, but he became an ardent convert to the faith upon being addressed by the disembodied voice of Jesus while on the road from Jerusalem to Damascus. Then after being baptized and adopting the 'Christian' name of Paul, he began preaching Christ's message, first in Palestine, where he had little success in converting his fellow Jews, and later, with considerably more success, in cities like Ephesus and Antioch in Asia Minor, whose inhabitants were mainly pagan Greeks, in Corinth and Thessalonica in Greece, and in Rome.

In AD 46 Paul and a fellow disciple named Barnabas, while preaching in the town of Iconium (now in present-day central Turkey), learned that the local Jews intended to stone them, so they were obliged to flee south to Lystra, a city in Lycaonia. There Paul miraculously healed a man who had been crippled since birth, and this caused the superstitious populace to believe that the heavily bearded Barnabas was the god Zeus and that the loquacious Paul was Hermes, even though they tried to convince them otherwise. But not long afterwards things took a decided turn for the worse:

And there came thither certain Jews from Antioch and Iconium, who persuaded the people, and, having stoned Paul, drew him out of the city, supposing him to be dead. Howbeit, as the disciples stood round about him, he rose up, and came into the city: and the next day he departed with Barnabus to Derbe. (*Acts*, XIV, 19–20)

Fourteen years later, in AD 60, writing his second letter to the Corinthians from Ephesus, Paul, after having described the various difficulties he had endured while proselytising in Asia Minor – he records that 'five times I was given the thirty-nine lashes by the Jews, three times I was whipped by the Romans, and once I was stoned' – goes on to mention the following experience:

I knew a man in Christ above fourteen years ago, (whether in the body, I cannot tell; or whether out of the body, I cannot tell: God knoweth;) such an one caught up to the third heaven. And I knew such a man, (whether in the body, or out of the body, I cannot tell: God knoweth;) how that he was caught up into paradise, and heard unspeakable words, which it is not lawful for a man to utter. Of such an one will I glory: yet of myself I will not glory, but in mine infirmities. (2 Corinthians, XII, 2–5)

As he had been stoned and left for dead in Lystra fourteen years before, his description of 'a man in Christ' who was taken up to the third heaven is almost certainly an account of what happened to him. If this supposition is right, Paul's stoning led to him having an NDE, in which he was apparently carried in his wraith form out of his body and up into the third heaven, where God himself resides. And although Paul did not reveal much about what he saw and heard there, it is evident that his excursion into the beyond was a truly wonderful and awe-inspiring event.

Paul's reticence in revealing more inspired others to fill the gap by writing accounts which supplied the missing details and which were fraudulently ascribed to him. The best known and important of these forged documents is the so-called *Apocalypse of Paul*. To give the work credibility, it was claimed that, following an angelic revelation, the manuscript was found during the reign of the Emperor Theodosius (ruled AD 378-95), lying in a marble box hidden under the floor of Paul's former home in Tarsus. However, the fifth-century church historian Hermias Sozomen said of the story: 'When I inquired about this, a Cilician, a priest of the church of Tarsus, told me it was a lie.' In fact, the *Apocalypse of Paul* was probably written not long before it first appeared. The text was known to St Augustine, who reputedly laughed at those gullible enough to believe it was genuine, although it was widely read and accepted by early Christians.

Before I consider what the *Apocalypse of Paul* says about the next life, it is important to mention one or two others of the many apocryphal works that appeared during the second, third and fourth centuries AD. These too were written by Christians who wished to satisfy the general yearning among their compatriots for more information about the life of Jesus and about the doings or 'acts' of apostles like Peter, Paul, Andrew and Thomas, and they included various gospels, epistles and apocalypses ascribed to them. And while much of their content is spurious and often badly written, they do contain some remarkable nuggets of fact, which had probably been obtained either from earlier manuscripts now lost or handed down by word of mouth. For example, in the so-called *Acts of Paul* (written about AD 160) we are given a description of what Paul looked like, which is so unflattering to him from a physical point of view that it is probably accurate: 'And he saw Paul coming, a man of little stature, thin-haired upon the head, crooked in the legs, of good state of body, with eyebrows joining, and nose somewhat hooked, full of grace: for sometimes he appeared like a man, and sometimes he had the face of an angel.'

One of the most astonishing occurrences is related in the second-century AD *Book of James*, also known as the *Protoevangelium*. The event reputedly happened to Joseph while he was travelling to Bethlehem with the heavily pregnant Mary (who rode upon an ass) to register for the census. When they were about 3 miles from the town, Mary started to go into labour, and Joseph, after laying her down in a cave beside the road, carried on in the hope of finding a midwife. But then suddenly – and the event is recorded in the first person, as if Joseph's actual words have been extracted from a lost journal and included in the text – it seemed to Joseph as if the world around him came to a stop, the flow of time becoming frozen at one moment, as in a photograph:

Now I Joseph was walking, and I walked not . . . And I looked up into the pole of heaven and saw it standing still, and the fowls of heaven without motion. And I looked upon the earth and saw a dish set, and workmen lying *by it*, and their hands were in the dish; and

JOURNEYS TO HEAVEN AND TO HELL ·

they that were chewing chewed not, and they that were lifting *the food* lifted it not, and they that put it to their mouth put it not thereto, but the faces of all of them were looking upward. And behold there were sheep being driven, and they went not forward but stood still: and the shepherd lifted his hand to smite them with his staff, and his hand remained up. And I looked upon the stream of the river and saw the mouths of the kids upon *the water* and they drank not. And of a sudden all things moved onward in their course.

What gives Joseph's experience a remarkable power is that while it precedes his meeting with a midwife and, not long afterwards, the birth of Jesus, it is not presented as being either an omen or a precursor of these events. Hence to Joseph it was a wonderful happening in its own right, which has on occasions been reported by mystics and which is called 'the timeless moment' by the poet T.S. Eliot.

The earliest apocalypse is that ascribed to Peter, and was written in about AD 120. It was influential in prompting the composition of similar texts, but particularly in giving us the first albeit brief description of paradise and graphically, and in far more detail, outlining the torments of hell.

The *Apocalypse of Peter* claims that Jesus once took his twelve disciples up on to a mountain to pray, whereupon they asked him to show them the appearance of the righteous after death. And soon afterwards, while they were praying,

There appeared two men standing before the Lord upon whom we were not able to look. For there issued from their countenance a ray as from the sun, and their raiment was shining so as the eye of man never saw the like: for no man is able to declare the glory wherewith they were clad and the beauty of their countenance.

Peter then drew near to Jesus and asked him about the place from whence they came.

And the Lord showed me a very great region outside this world exceeding bright with light, and the air of that place illuminated

76

with the beams of the sun, and the earth of itself flowering with blossoms that fade not, and full of spices and plants, fair-flowering and incorruptible, and bearing blessed fruit. And so great was the blossom that the odour thereof was borne thence ever to us. And the dwellers in that place were clad with the raiment of shining angels. And the angels ran round about them there. And the glory of them that dwelt there was all equal, and with one voice they praised the Lord God, rejoicing in that place.

Hence the wraiths of the righteous dead were taken to a wonderful garden or paradise, one similar indeed to that seen by Gilgamesh and by Heracles, and seemingly identical to the Elysian Fields of the Greeks. Yet the garden did not lie under the earth or indeed on its surface, but was instead placed somewhere 'outside this world', which suggests that its location was in the sky. Today we would probably prefer to think that if it does exist, it lies in an altogether different dimension of being, one that is spiritual, not physical.

The *Apocalypse of Peter* therefore seems to proclaim the idea, which, as we have seen, originated at least as early as the lifetime of Socrates, that there is a place 'outside this world' to which the good and righteous are taken after death, although it also indicates that this paradise is reserved for the followers of Christ. This was of crucial importance in view of the fact that whereas Jesus had often spoken of the coming kingdom of heaven and said that its advent would be sudden and unexpected, he also claimed it would occur during the lifetime of people then living. But much to the confusion and disappointment of his followers the prophecy was not fulfilled, which created a growing problem for them as time went by. Indeed, Peter says the reason why he and the other apostles asked Jesus to show them what departed Christians looked like was so that 'we might ... take courage, and encourage also the men that *should* hear us'. The difficulty was also conveniently dealt with in part by reinterpreting the parables about the kingdom of heaven, which by their nature are difficult to understand, as symbolizing the growth of the

Christian Church. Thus the mustard seed, for example, was taken to represent Jesus, from whom came his Church, which would eventually grow and spread to all parts of the world and so create the kingdom of heaven on earth.

The prospect of the imminent arrival of the kingdom of heaven had not only created a sense of urgent expectancy among early Christians, but it had also stimulated them to follow Christ's teachings more rigorously and devoutly, while at the same time helping them to attract more converts to the faith. But as its immediacy receded, it became necessary to find a substitute that would offer the same advantages to Christians. And this is what the *Apocalypse of Peter* so successfully did by holding out the prospect of a heavenly place 'outside this world' after death for good Christians, while displaying the torments of hell to those who might be tempted to stray or who were pagan non-believers. Thus heaven or paradise became the tempting carrot, while hell was the threatening stick.

The *Apocalypse of Paul* goes one important step further by representing paradise as being located in heaven, although it does so on a sounder basis, for it purports to relate what Paul actually saw and heard there. But its longer text is at least partly based on the *Apocalypse of Peter*, which in some respects accords with the experiences of those in later times who clinically died. But whether this means the author of the *Apocalypse of Peter* makes use of an actual NDE when he describes what Peter was shown by Jesus, or if such people have unconsciously recalled his writings, must remain for the moment an open question.

The *Apocalypse of Paul* says that when Paul's wraith arrived in the third heaven, it was addressed by the voice of 'the Lord', which told Paul among other things that each day, at sunrise and sunset, the guardian angels of all the world's inhabitants assembled before him to impart the good or bad things that their respective human charges had done. Then later, Paul was shown the appearance of the angels who escorted wraiths into God's spiritual presence when the phys-

78

ical body died. Those guiding the just were compassionate angels who wore golden girdles and had faces that shone like the sun. The unmerciful angels leading the unjust, however, had furious faces and brightly shining eyes, and from their hair and mouths burst sparks of fire. Each wraith was individually brought by them before God to be judged, and depending upon how he or she had behaved in life, was sent by him either to paradise or to the 'place of torment'.

Not long afterwards Paul asked his angelic guide if he might be shown what those two regions were like. The angel assented, saying first: 'Follow me again, and I will show thee the place of the righteous where they are taken.'

And I followed the angel and he took me up unto the third heaven and set me before the door of a gate; and I looked on it and saw, and the gate was of gold, and there were two pillars of gold full of golden letters; and the angel turned again to me and said: Blessed art thou if thou enterest in by these gates, for it is not permitted to any to enter save only to those that have kept goodness and pureness of their bodies in all things. And I asked the angel and said: Lord, tell me for what cause are these letters set upon these tables? The angel answered and said unto me: These are the names of the righteous that minister unto God with their whole heart, which dwell on the earth . . .

On entering the golden gates, Paul was warmly greeted by none other than Enoch, an aged man whose face also shone like the sun, and by Elijah, although both quickly began to weep at the amount of sin still being committed in the world. Then, after being told by the angel to reveal nothing of what he saw and heard, Paul was conducted around the interior of that holy place, which allowed the author to mention the famous phrase from the real Paul's letter to the Corinthians, to wit, that Paul 'heard unspeakable things, which it is not lawful for a man to utter'.

Entry into the third heaven was therefore granted only to good Christians who remained celibate or 'pure'. This perhaps explains why becoming a monk or a nun became so popular in later times, as only they could realistically hope for the ultimate in celestial acceptance, although both virgins and couples who had entered into what was considered a true Christian marriage – living together in a chaste manner, which was of course equally difficult to do – would also be welcomed there.

Next Paul not only saw 'a river flowing with milk and honey', beside which grew numerous trees laden with fruit and vines heavy with grapes, much as Peter had witnessed in the paradise shown to him by Jesus, but also a lake called Acherusa, whose waters were whiter than milk. Then, accompanied by 3,000 angels singing a hymn, he was rowed across the lake in a golden ship, which carried him to the city of Christ. The city was surrounded by twelve concentrically arranged golden walls, each of which had a gate and a tower. The walls were 1 furlong or 220 yards apart, thus giving a distance from the outer wall to the city centre, if we disregard the unknown thickness of each wall, of 1 mile and 660 yards, which is a walk of about twenty-five minutes. Four rivers – 'a river of honey called Phison, and the river of milk Euphrates, and the river of oil Geon, and the river of wine Tigris' – flowed alongside the outer wall on each side of the city, which reveal it to have been square in shape.

Before the city's outer gate (or possibly between the gates, the text is unclear) stood tall, fruitless trees, among which loitered weeping men who were not allowed to go any further. These were Christians who had taken pride in their good acts. Paul was then conducted to each river in turn, on whose banks lived the wraiths of righteous Jews. Thus beside the river of honey, to which the prophets went, he came across Ezekiel, Amos, Zacharias and other biblical seers, while beside the river of milk, the home of the chaste, he met the children killed by King Herod. The wraiths of those who had been hospitable to strangers resided beside the river of wine, where Paul encountered Abraham, Isaac and Jacob, amongst others. And those who had praised God without pride went to the river of oil, where he saw many unnamed wraiths 'rejoicing and singing psalms'. Paul learned that these right-eous Jews would all eventually be admitted into the city of Christ.

Paul was next led through each of the twelve gates, and he noticed to his surprise many wraiths seated beside them on golden thrones and wearing crowns of gold and other jewels. He was told that they were all Christians with goodness and understanding in their hearts, but that they had 'made them-selves foolish for the Lord God's sake, knowing neither the Scriptures nor many psalms'. On reaching the centre of the city of Christ, Paul saw there an altar 'exceeding high', beside which stood King David of Israel, whose face also shone like the sun, holding 'a psaltery and a harp' and singing 'Allelulia' in a voice loud enough to fill the entire city. When Paul asked why David alone of the Jews was there, he was given a star-tling and revealing reply: 'When Christ the Son of God sitteth on the right hand of his Father,' said the angel, 'this David shall sing praises before him in the seventh heaven: and as it is done in the heavens, so likewise is it below.'

Thus here, at a stroke, the fictitious Paul reveals that there are seven heavens. Hence God does not reside, as the Jews supposed, in the third heaven with his angels, but rather in the highest or seventh heaven, where Jesus has since joined him. The third heaven has now become the location of paradise, where the wraiths of righteous Christians and Jews go after death, although only the former are allowed into the city of Christ. And at Judgement Day, when the world is destroyed, the righteous resurrected will also be taken into this 'land of promise' to live, 'and then shall the Lord Jesus Christ the eter-nal king be manifested and shall come with all his saints to dwell therein; and he shall reign over them for a thousand years.'

But while this description of heaven and its golden gates is an attractive and plausible concept, the city of Christ and its surroundings are really a celestial version of the Greek under-world. The Greeks, as we have noted, associated three with death, which explains why 'Paul' places paradise in the third heaven. The beautiful parkland around the city of Christ, with its numerous heavily laden fruit trees and vines, resembles not only the interior of Elysium but also the western gardens visited by Heracles and Gilgamesh. The city of Christ lies near to a river of milk and honey and is bounded by four rivers and a lake, just as Hades is by the Styx and its five tributaries. The lake is called Acherusa, which derives from the name of one of the Styx's tributaries, the Acheron, meaning 'stream of woe'. Passage across both Lake Acherusa and the River Styx is by boat, although we are not told who rows or sails it across the lake. Those wraiths without a coin to pay Charon, or whose bodies lie unburied, are left stranded on the bank of the Styx in the same way that righteous Jews must remain outside the city beside their respective rivers. The city is surrounded by twelve high walls made of gold, and Tartarus is encircled by one made of bronze. Entry to both is via their gates. And when Jesus, the third aspect of the Christian Trinity of Father, Son and Holy Ghost, descends at Judgement Day from the seventh heaven to reside in the third, where he will judge both 'the quick and the dead', he will replicate the descent of Hades, the third of three divine brothers, into the underworld to become its king.

4
The Torments of Hell

My name is on thy roll, and sure I must
Increase thy gloomy kingdom in the dust.
My soul at this no apprehension feels,
But trembles at thy swords, thy racks, thy wheels.

From *To Death* by Lady Winchilsea

The English word 'hell', which we give to the supposed under-world where the wraiths of sinners are punished, is derived from the name of an obscure Teutonic goddess. She was Hel, the daughter of Loki, who according to legend became the ruler of some of the dead after being banished to the nether regions by Odin. The latter, like the Greek deity Hermes, was the god of trade, travel and magic, as well being the *psychopompos* ('soul-guide') or conductor of the dead, although this task he generally left to fierce female spirits called Valkyries. Odin also presided over the Teutonic paradise of Valhalla, the blessed opposite of Hel's dreary realm. In appearance, Hel was represented as an ugly, blonde-haired woman, whose large-nosed face was half black and bore a merciless, harsh expression. Half of her body was also said to resemble raw flesh.

The domain of Hel, called Niflheim (or 'mist-world') or Hela, resembled the underworld of the Greeks and Mesopotamians in being dark and dismal. In early times it was thought to be very cold, which made it unpleasant for its inmates and quite different from the Christian hell, which is reputedly very hot. Only later, following the introduction of Christianity into northern Europe, was it represented as being fiery, as Sigvar the Scald, for example, reveals in his poetic address to King (later Saint) Olav of Norway (AD 995–1030):

> Thronged was the way to heaven
> Against those who betrayed their lord,
> And they who worked the treason
> Will seek Hel, the fire's deep home.

Niflheim was similarly described as being surrounded by a strong wall, which had a mighty gate. The gate was reached by journeying along a road, and it was guarded, like that of Hades, by a dog, Garm, which chased away any live person who might seek to enter. In its earliest conception Hel's subterranean realm was not a place of torment or punishment, but was instead where the wraiths went of those who had lived ordinary, unheroic lives, and who had therefore died from such mundane causes as old age, disease or accident.

The wraiths of warriors, by contrast, who were expected to die gloriously in battle, went to Valhalla, Odin's domain and the equivalent of the Greek Elysium, where they lived the sort of life that living warriors regarded as ideal, to wit endlessly hunting, fighting and feasting, and generally having a masculine good time. Women's wraiths were also allowed into Valhalla if they had died in a suitably heroic manner by committing suicide and joining their slain warrior husbands on their funeral pyres, or by allowing themselves to be sacrificed to Odin.

I have noted that the pagan Greeks did not regard Tartarus as being particularly hot, except insofar as it was surrounded by a river of fire called Phlegethon, a tributary of the Styx, whose purpose, like the wall it bordered, was to prevent those inside escaping. The same is true of the early Mesopotamian underworld, which was predominantly dusty and where punishment for the errant rich and powerful consisted of being reduced to the level of servants, or as was later supposed, by being flogged, flayed and beaten, or even eaten, by ugly winged demons. The wraiths of ordinary folk who had sinned against the gods were also tortured, although for most the mere fact of being confined in a dark, dusty and dismal place, from which there was little hope of reprieve, was punishment enough.

The underworld as conceived by the early Egyptians, known as Duat, was unusual in not always being dark, for it apparently had a river named Urnes running through it, along which the ship carrying the sun-god Ra sailed at night. The voyage below ground enabled the deity to reach the eastern horizon by morning, from whence he could again rise into the sky. Thus like Egypt itself, Duat had alternating twelve-hour periods of light and darkness.

The wraiths of the dead were believed to enter Duat via the same western opening as the river Urnes, which they reached by making a long and hazardous journey across the Sahara desert. Once inside the underworld, they were individually brought naked before Osiris, the god of the dead, who judged each by weighing his or her heart (wherein resided, it was thought, the person's consciousness and will) against the goddess Maat or truth. Those who failed the test were sliced into pieces by knife-wielding serpents. No rebirth was therefore possible for the wicked. The good and the just, however, received their reward by being sent to the field of Aalu, which like Elysium, Dilmun, Valhalla, and the Isles of the Blessed, was a blissful, sunny domain without famine or sickness, whose inhabitants lived happily doing what had most pleased them in life. Those who had been neither good nor bad, on the other hand, were destined, after a suitable sojourn in Duat, to be reborn.

In *The Histories*, Herodotus records a story told to him in Egypt about how Rhampsinitus, its second king, had once physically descended into the underworld, as Heracles is said to have done, where he played dice with Demeter, 'sometimes winning and sometimes losing, and returned to earth with a golden napkin which she had given him as a present'. Since the Egyptians founded a festival to mark Rhampsinitus's descent into and return from Duat, which was still commemorated in Herodotus' day, we can be reasonably sure that something extraordinary happened to him. The clue is provided by the fact that he played dice, not with Demeter, a Greek goddess, but rather with Isis, the consort of Osiris and the goddess of the dead, whose introduction of cereal cultivation into Egypt identified her in the Greek mind with Demeter.

This in fact suggests that Rhampsinitus once suffered from a dangerous ailment that brought him, not once but several times, to the brink of death, and which may have resulted in his wraith leaving his body on each occasion and departing to the next realm, only to return as he regained consciousness. The alternating lapses of consciousness and periods of wakefulness were thereafter symbolized by him 'playing dice with death', which game he eventually won as he fully recovered, just as his wraith's separations became conceptualized as a physical descent into the nether regions.

The Christian notion that hell is a hot, fiery place did not come about, as might be supposed, from the observation of molten lava emerging from volcanic vents, but instead was inherited from Jewish beliefs in such a place, although its reality would have been suitably confirmed by such extrusions from below ground. As we have noted, the early Jews thought that the wraiths of the dead all went to the same underground repository or 'pit' named Sheol, where according to one school of thought they lay in a state of complete immobility, much as the body does in the grave. According to the other, they wandered about listlessly in the darkness like shadows. The latter idea, as well as the notion that Sheol lay underground, was supported by the raising of the wraith of Samuel by the witch of Endor. King Saul, who was threatened by the Philistines, asked the witch to do this, in order that he might consult with his former mentor, who had died five years earlier (in 1061 BC). The witch at first refused, knowing that Saul had expelled or killed other witches and wizards, but was assured that no harm would come to her.

And the king said unto her, Be not afraid: for what sawest thou? And the woman said unto Saul, I saw gods ascending out of the earth. And he said unto her, What form is he of? And she said, An old man cometh up; and he *is* covered with a mantle. And Saul perceived that it *was* Samuel, and he stooped with *his* face to the ground, and bowed himself. (*I Samuel,* I, 13–14)

The fact that Samuel's wraith was then able to speak to Saul just as he had in life reveals that he still possessed consciousness and self-awareness, although his prophecy that Saul would be defeated and killed, along with his sons, the next day – 'And tomorrow *shalt* thou and thy sons *be* with me' – brought no comfort to the worried king.

During the following centuries the layout of Sheol underwent a transformation in Jewish thinking. From being a vast, utterly dark underground chamber where all the dead went, irrespective of what they had done in life, it became subdivided on moral grounds into four regions, two of which were reserved for the righteous (or good) and two for the unrighteous (or bad). Of the first two regions, one was a blissful, light-filled abode, like Elysium, where the wraiths of the martyrs resided, and the other a somewhat less pleasant area where the righteous who had not been martyred lived. Of the other two, one was for the wraiths of sinners who had been wealthy and influential in life, the other for those from a lower stratum of society, who had been caught doing wrong when alive and punished for their crimes. Later, as we discovered when we considered Jesus' parable about Lazarus and the rich man, the two regions for the good were united into one, which thereby became a subterranean heaven and took the name Sheol, while the two for the bad were similarly combined to form what became the blueprint for the Christian hell, and was called Gehenna. We do not know if these changes were based on the direct observation of those who had had a NDE, or occurred because they gave to the just and God-fearing some hope of a reward after death, while holding out the prospect of post-mortem punishment as a preventative to those who were tempted to do wrong.

Likewise, the darkness of the original Sheol was confined

to the two regions of the damned, but their unpleasantness was then made worse by the addition of fire, wherein sinners were burned. This important and novel change was naturally carried over into the unified chamber, although it was fiercely debated whether or not the flames emitted light. Its name Gehenna gives the origin of this grim conception, for it derives from the valley or ravine of Hinnom (or Ge-Hinnom, now called Wadi er-Rababeh), situated to the west of Jerusalem. The ravine had in early times gained a dire reputation because the Canaanite worshippers of Moloch once sacrificed first-born children there. And later, the Jews used it to incinerate rubbish, along with the corpses of animals and executed felons. In fact it was said that the contents of Ge-Hinnom were continually aflame and noxiously smoking, and it must have presented what we would today call a 'truly hellish' scene.

The first detailed portrait of the Christian hell occurs in the *Apocalypse of Peter*. After describing the view of paradise shown to him by Jesus, the author continues by saying: 'And I saw also another place over against that one, very squalid: and it was a place of torment, and they that were punished and the angels that punished them had their raiment dark, according to the air of the place.'

However, the work's placement of hell 'over against' paradise lying 'outside this world' suggests that the two are close together, which would mean that hell is also outside this world, although the Christian hell, like the pagan underworld, has always been envisaged as lying below ground. This indicates that the writer of the *Apocalypse of Peter*, who was probably a Greek Christian, is trying to square the eschatological circle by implying that the paradise of Christians is somewhere apart from this world, without committing the sacrilege of placing it in the sky and thereby parting it completely from the 'place of torment'. For after all, Jesus himself had said in the parable of Lazarus and the rich man that the two were within hailing distance of one another.

This seemingly impossible but none the less necessary task

was completed by whoever wrote the *Apocalypse of Paul*. For, while drawing upon the descriptions of paradise and hell given in the *Apocalypse of Peter* and similar works, he cleverly uses the out-of-body experience of Paul, who had almost single-handedly founded the Christian church, to put paradise in the third heaven, although he rather strangely moves hell at the same time by representing it as lying in the far west where the sun sets.

The punishments that Peter was shown being inflicted in the 'place of torment' differed according to the crimes that the victims had committed when alive. Most of them involved some form of burning, although in one case those concerned were tormented by 'worms'. This fully accords with Jewish ideas about the goings-on in Gehenna, which were in turn based on the fires and the worm-eaten (or more correctly, maggot-eaten) corpses at Ge-Hinnom.

Thus the wraiths of people who had 'blasphemed the way of righteousness' were suspended by their tongues over bonfires, while formerly adulterous females were held above them by their hair. The men who had fornicated with such women were hung upside down by their feet, with their heads dipped in boiling mud. Those who had borne false witness had fire continually poured into their mouths; moneylenders were stood up to their knees in a boiling mixture of blood, pus and mud; and anyone who had forsaken the way of God was fried in a pan like a kipper. However, the wraiths of murderers were 'cast into a strait place full of evil, creeping things, and smitten by those beasts', which included being set upon by dark clouds of worms. And whereas women who had aborted their children were stood up to their necks in a foul-smelling lake, homosexuals and lesbians were thrown over a rocky precipice, forced to make their way to the top again, and then cast down when they got there, *ad infinitum*, in a punishment somewhat resembling that of Sisyphus.

In a version of the *Apocalypse of Peter* found in Ethiopia, the various types of punishment are represented as occurring in separate pits. The souls of the damned were taken to them, and their punishment supervised by angels of God, suitably dressed in dark clothing, of whom the two most important were named Ezraël and Uriel. Indeed, it is interesting to note that at this early date there is no mention of the Devil, nor of Satan or Beelzebub, nor of demons. Thus the 'place of torment' was originally considered to have been directly established by God for the punishment of sinners, and he then left its day-to-day running to certain of his angels. However, the writer of the *Apocalypse of Paul* takes the situation a step closer to the one with which we are familiar today, as he calls the angelic supervisors 'evil angels'. These were directed, he says, by an overseer appropriately named Tataruchus, from whom they obtain their collective name of Tartaruchi.

Another second-century apocryphal work, the *Acts of Thomas*, describes the travels of, and the miracles performed by, that apostle after Christ's departure into heaven. It is the source of Thomas's supposed missionary journey to India, where it says he converted and baptized King Gundaphorus and his brother Gad into the faith. King Gundaphorus is an historical figure, the ruler (from AD 19 to 46) of a large semi-autonomous eastern province of the Parthian empire, which extended from what is now Afghanistan, through northern Pakistan to the Punjab of India, although there is no direct evidence to show that he was a convert to Christianity or that Thomas actually went to the subcontinent. But the fact that Gundaphorus and his brother Gad are mentioned in the *Acts of Thomas*, along with the known early presence of Christian sects in north-eastern India and the existence of what is claimed to be Thomas's tomb in Mylapore, suggest that he might well have done. If so, he would have visited Taxila, the capital of Gundaphorus's kingdom, which was situated on the upper Indus River not far south of the Khyber Pass.

The sixth act or miracle attributed to Thomas in the *Acts of Thomas* is of particular interest, as it concerns the resuscitation of a young Indian woman from death, who, unlike those similarly revived in both the Old and New Testaments, was able to recall what she saw in the nether regions. The

circumstances of her death are bizarre. She had fallen in love
with a handsome young man who reciprocated her feelings,
but he, having become a devout Christian, asked her to
'become my consort in chastity and pure conversation', a
demand to which she naturally objected. However, fearing
that she might 'pollute' herself with another (and doubtless
jealous that she would), the youth killed her with a sword.

Following the shrivelling of his hands when taking the
Eucharist, the young man confessed his crime to Thomas
who, after decrying his murderous act, helped him to revive
the dead woman. The apostle, knowing that her lusts had
certainly caused her to be taken to hell, asked her to relate her
experiences there. She began by mentioning her guide:

A man took me who was hateful to look upon, altogether black,
and his raiment exceedingly foul, and he took me away to a place
wherein were many pits, and a great stench and hateful odour
issued thence. And he caused me to look into every pit, and I saw
in the first pit flaming fire, and wheels of fire ran round there, and
souls were hanged upon those wheels, and were dashed against
each other; and very great crying and howling was there, and
there was none to deliver.

The woman was therefore shown a 'place of torment'
which is hot and fiery like that seen by Peter, including the
numerous pits mentioned in the Ethiopian version of his
Apocalypse. But whether this similarity can be taken as
confirmation of Peter's supposed experience or simply means
that the writer of the *Acts of Thomas* drew upon the same
work is an open question. We certainly find a remarkable
correspondence between the two works in what the young
woman saw in one pit: 'Another pit he showed me, where-
into I stooped and looked and saw souls hanging, some by
the tongue, some by the hair, some by the hands, and some
head downwards by the feet, and tormented with smoke and
brimstone.'

The sins prompting punishment in this manner, however,

were arguably less serious than those described by 'Peter'. This suggests that the author is reflecting the shift in opinion that occurred in the period between the writing of the two works, with honesty, modesty and clean living taking pride of place as behavioural ideals:

The souls which are hanged by the tongue are slanderers, that uttered lying and shameful words, and were not ashamed; and they that are hanged by the hair are unblushing ones which had no modesty and went about the world bareheaded; and they that are hanged by the hands, these are they that took away and stole other men's goods . . . and they that hang upside down by the feet, these are they that lightly and readily ran in evil ways and disorderly paths, not visiting the sick nor escorting them that depart this life, and therefore each and every soul receiveth that which was done by it.

In the two centuries separating the writing of the *Acts of Thomas* and the *Apocalypse of Paul*, when both the popularity of Christianity and the importance of the Church grew considerably, a problem peculiar to the faith – namely the inappropriate behaviour of both church ministers and churchgoers – became of increasing concern, as did the sexual indiscretions of unmarried Christian women and of married couples. Pagans had always had a fairly free-and-easy attitude to sex, but such liberality was condemned as sinful by the Church, which actively sought to encourage purity in both mind and body – as indeed Christ himself had done. This explains why many of the sinners supposedly seen in hell by Paul during his out-of-body state were people who had let their lusts lead them astray, including several Church officials. Yet oddly, while the punishment meted out to fornicators and to the slipshod and mocking is invariably horrible and fiery, there is no mention of anyone there who had committed far more serious crimes like violent assault or murder. Hence the *Apocalypse of Paul* primarily served the Church by presenting a tempting reward in its depiction of the glory of heaven to

those who lived truly Christian lives, while offering a terrify-
ing portrayal of everlasting torment to the feckless, disre-
spectful and immoral. It was left to the poet Edmund Waller
(1606–87) to observe:

> The fear of hell, or aiming to be blest,
> Savours too much of private interest.

The fictitious Paul was led from heaven by his angelic
guide, who took him 'by the way of the sunsetting' and
showed him a view of what appeared to be a 'great river'
below. When he asked the angel what the river was, he was
told: 'This is the ocean which compasseth the whole earth
about.' 'Paul' continues by saying: 'And when I was come
beyond the ocean, I looked and there was no light in that
place, but darkness and sorrow and sadness: and I sighed.'
This disclosure is both strange and revealing, for the 'place of
torment' is apparently no longer underground but rather
beyond the Ocean Stream, which indicates that the author is
drawing upon earlier ideas equating the western ocean with
the 'waters of death'. But then instead of placing some paradisial equivalent of Dilmun beyond them, he mixes everything
up by making it the location of hell. Furthermore, because we
know that there is no Ocean Stream 'which compasseth the
whole earth', but rather towards the west is the Atlantic
Ocean across which lies the continent of North America, we
also learn that it is not a genuine view of the earth as seen from
a great height, but is instead nothing more than an imaginative
description written by someone conversant with the geography of the world as described by Hecatæus. This likewise
suggests that the author of the *Apocalypse of Paul* was a Greek
Christian and probably also a pagan convert.

The question of the whereabouts of hell, which is puzzling
when we consider the conflicting claims of the popular
Apocalypse of Paul and the traditional belief that Hades lies
below ground, was discussed by St Gregory in his *Dialogues*,
written in AD 593, three years after he became Pope. He says:

Touching this point I dare not rashly define anything: for some have been of opinion that hell was in some place upon earth; and others think that it is under the earth: but then this doubt ariseth, for if it be therefore called hell, or an infernal place, because it is below, then as the earth is distant from heaven, so likewise should hell be distant from the earth: for which cause, perhaps, the Prophet saith: *Thou hast delivered my soul from the lower hell* (*Psalm* 86, 13); so that the higher hell may seem to be upon the earth, and the lower under the earth . . .

Hence for St Gregory there are probably two hells, an upper and a lower, which nicely solved the problem, although later hell was placed squarely back underground, and its geography based, or so it seems, on the intermediate Jewish concept of a joint four-chambered Sheol/Gehenna. The lowest was hell proper, the next purgatory, then limbo, and lastly the 'limbo of the Fathers', where resided the wraiths of good pagans who had lived before the coming of Christ and which resembled, in effect, the Greek Elysium.

The predominant feature of the ficticious Paul's above-ground 'place of torment' was a river of fire 'burning with heat', wherein a great multitude of wraiths was immersed, some up to their knees, some up to their navels, some up to their lips, and the remainder up to their eyebrows. All of them, 'Paul' was informed, had while alive committed offences of a religious or moral nature, although these, when judged by present-day standards, seem comparatively mild in comparison to the ghastliness of their punishment. Thus those standing up to their knees in the river of fire had merely engaged in idle talk when emerging from church, while those submerged up to their navels were guilty of having had sex after taking communion. And likewise, the wraiths immersed up to their lips were guilty of nothing worse than slandering each other when in church, and those almost fully bathed in the fiery river had beckoned to one another in church and, somewhat more seriously, had plotted evil against their neighbours.

'Paul' was then shown the punishments inflicted on certain individual Church ministers who had behaved improperly. The first, a priest, had been found guilty of 'eating and drinking and whoring' while standing before God's altar. He was dragged by the throat to the river of fire, stood up to his knees in it, and then stabbed with a three-pronged iron fork in his abdomen by one of the evil angels. The second, a bishop, had shown no compassion to widows and orphans. He was made to run to the river of fire, immersed in it up to his knees, and then severely beaten with stones about the face and body. The third, a deacon, had both eaten church food offerings and 'committed fornication'. He was likewise stood up to his knees in the river of fire, whereupon worms wriggled out from his mouth and nostrils. The last, a church reader, had failed to keep God's commandments. He too was placed in the river of fire, and then had his lips and mouth cut with a red-hot razor wielded by one of the evil angels.

Similarly, those who had failed to pay attention in church and who had laughed at the proceedings were punished in a special pit surrounded by a wall and a river of fire, where they were made to chew their lips and tongues. Separate pits also contained wrongdoers like usurers, adulterers, naughty girls, fast breakers, magicians and sorcerers, sodomites, women who had aborted their children, heathens and Christian hypocrites, all of whom were being horribly tortured. It is perhaps only necessary to mention what happened to the girls who had engaged in pre-marital sex behind their parents' backs. Clad in black clothes, these were individually led away with red-hot chains looped around their necks by 'four fearful angels' into darkness and an unknown fate. The depth of one pit, into which were thrown the wraiths of those who refused to believe in Christ, was given as 3,000 cubits, or about 4,500 feet, which suggests that the Church was becoming increasingly frustrated and annoyed at the strong and continuing resistance shown by many pagans to conversion.

One punishment, however, is quite different from the others and is of special interest. It reads:

And I looked and saw others hanging over a channel of water, and their tongues were exceeding dry, and many fruits were set in their sight, and they were not suffered to take them. And I asked: Who are these, Lord? And he said to me: These are they that brake the fast before the time appointed: therefore without ceasing do they pay this penalty.

This is nothing other than the punishment which was inflicted upon Tantalus in Greek myth. Tantalus, the king of either Argos or Corinth, had apparently somehow become such a good friend of Zeus that the latter invited him to dine with him and the other gods on Mount Olympus, an honour granted to few mortals. However, not only did Tantalus betray the secrets he heard and steal some of the divine food, but when he was obliged to return the lavish hospitality and found that the palace larder did not contain sufficient meat, he made up the shortfall by cutting up and cooking his son Pelops. But the disgusting ingredient was soon divinely detected, and Tantalus was angrily killed by Zeus. His wraith was sent to Tartarus, where it was endlessly tormented by hunger and thirst in the manner described above. Such a borrowing reveals that the author of the *Apocalypse of Paul*, having plagiarized the *Apocalypse of Peter* but needing other horrors to serve as a warning to lax Christians, used his evident knowledge of Greek myths to fabricate an appropriate punishment for those who prematurely ended their fasts.

The breaking of fasts, which meant in effect failing in one's duty to God, was a serious offence in ancient times. This is perhaps why the Talmud contains the story of a certain holy man who saw in a vision the punishments inflicted on those in Gehenna, one of whom was a woman named Miriam. She had been guilty of fasting for a day and then blasphemously overeating on the following two days. For this sin, the vision revealed, she was suspended by her nipples over flames. Another Miriam, a teacher, was taken prematurely to Gehenna by mistake. The assistant of the angel of death, it was said, should have brought down the wraith of a hairdresser named Miriam to the underworld, but was misled by the name, and carried down that of Miriam the teacher instead. When the error was pointed out to him, the assistant said he would rectify it by returning Miriam's wraith to her body, to which the angel of death replied, 'Since you have brought her, let her be reckoned among the dead.'

This was unusual, as the victims of such mistakes are usually returned to their bodies and come back to life. They are then able to report on what happened to them. Two further examples of near fatal mix-ups involving people with the same name are considered later on.

Finally, in view of what some have claimed to have seen in hell during an NDE, it is pertinent to note that although the imaginary Paul's 'place of torment' was hot and fiery and most of the punishments involved burning, the *Apocalypse* rather surprisingly mentions two pits which contained ice and snow and which were therefore very cold. In one of them sinners who 'had injured the fatherless and widows and the poor' lay naked with their hands and feet cut off, while worms ate them. In the other, which was even colder, men and women stood shivering and gnashing their teeth, and were harried by two-headed worms a cubit long. Apparently, these sinners were paying the penalty for denying that Christ rose from the dead and that the dead would return to life on Judgement Day.

The existence of a fiery underworld where sinners are punished is referred to by Jesus in the New Testament, but only in a very general way. For example, in *Matthew*, XVIII, 8, he warns: 'And if thy eye offend thee, pluck it out, and cast it from thee: it is better for thee to enter into life with one eye, rather than having two eyes to be cast into hell fire.' But Jesus would not have spoken of 'hell', which was a word unknown at the time and which is simply the English version of the Aramaic one he would have used, namely Gehinnam, or the Hebrew Gehenna. This is made plain in Mark's version of the incident, for he has Jesus add, 'Where their worm dieth not, and the fire is not quenched.' This is an obvious reference to

Gehenna, whose two principal frights, as we have noted, are fire and worms.

Greek and Roman converts to Christianity, like their pagan fellow citizens, would have naturally referred to the underworld as Hades, which takes its name from its eponymous ruler, or as Tartarus. Jesus himself was probably familiar with both names, and indeed some modern translations of St Luke's Gospel have him using the former when he narrates the parable of Lazarus and the rich man, saying of the latter, 'He was in great pain in Hades.' But it gradually became clear to Christians that by keeping Hades, a pagan deity, as the underworld's king or ruler they were compromising their beliefs. After all, pagan deities were not supposed to exist, so if one was recognized as a real entity doing a worthwhile job, then it would be very hard to deny the existence of Hermes, who guided the dead, and of Persephone, or indeed to argue against giving some of the others responsibility for certain areas of life. But everybody knew the underworld had to have a ruler, just as earthly kingdoms did, so some means had to be found of dispensing with Hades and replacing him with an acceptable Christian alternative.

How this was done is outlined in another apocryphal work entitled the *Questions of Bartholomew*, which purports to record the questions about the underworld put by the apostle Bartholomew to the resurrected Jesus. The earliest extant text, which is in Greek, dates from the fifth century AD, but the work is certainly of earlier origin.

The *Questions of Bartholomew* begins by relating how Jesus miraculously vanished from the cross during the three-hour long eclipse which occurred during the crucifixion. His disappearance was, however, noticed by Bartholomew, who was standing nearby, and when he asked the resurrected Jesus where he went during that time, Jesus replied: 'I went down to Hades that I might bring up Adam and all them that were with him, according to the supplication of Michael the archangel.'

Jesus was not physically translocated straight to the underworld. He manifested instead at the top of a long flight of steps leading down there, and while he was descending the first 500 of them, Hades detected his approach and, frightened, cried out that a god was coming. Then as he walked down the next 500 steps, the angels accompanying Jesus commanded Hades to open the gates, whereupon Beliar or Death tried to calm his master by suggesting that it was probably only Elias or Enoch who was approaching. Hades dismissed this proposal, saying it was too soon for either of them to reappear on earth. He then felt a great pain internally, whereupon Jesus entered the gates of the underworld, took hold of him, scourged him and 'bound him with chains that cannot be loosed, and brought from thence all the patriarchs and came again to the cross.'

In this dramatic way Jesus effectively outperformed the mighty Greek hero Heracles, who had also 'harrowed Hades', although he had only released the imprisoned Theseus and brought Cerberus up from there. Jesus, by contrast, not only set free Adam and several other patriarchs, who were immediately carried to heaven by angels, but overcame Hades himself. Hades, however, left his name behind him, for Christians still referred to the underworld as Hades, even though this was in due course replaced by phrases like the 'place of torment' and then, much later, by the name 'hell'. And although he was bound and no longer the ruler of hell, Hades had such a grip on the ancient mind that according to St John's *Revelation* he will be released with the fourth horseman of the apocalypse, who is Death, and that 'power was given unto them over a fourth part of the earth, to kill with sword, and with hunger, and with death, and with the beasts of the earth'.

The *Questions of Bartholomew* goes on to say that when Jesus some time later took Peter and the other apostles to the Mount of Olives, Bartholomew asked Jesus to show him 'the adversary of men that we may behold him, of what fashion he is, and what is his work'. This gave Jesus the opportunity to introduce the new ruler of hell, who was none other than

Beliar (or Belial). At the Lord's command, he was brought up, bound in chains, by Michael and 600 other angels, 'and his face was like lightning and his eyes full of darkness. And out of his nostrils came a stinking smoke.' Beliar was also of immense size, with a height approaching 2,500 feet, and possessed of vast wings.

Bartholomew and the other apostles were terrified by this huge being, even though Beliar was laid out, chained and helpless, on the ground. Jesus then instructed Bartholomew to place his foot on the neck of the prone giant and ask him whatever questions he liked. The reluctant Bartholomew did this, pressing Beliar's face into the dirt and telling him to explain his origins. He was, he said, the first angel created by God (the second was Michael), and he was originally called Satanael, although since becoming the keeper of hell or Tartarus, he had borne the name of Satanas (or Satan). He further explained that although he was the first angel, he revolted against God when he, who was made by God from divine fire, was required to worship Adam, the first man, who was created in God's image out of humble earth. Thus pride was the cause of Satanael's fall. He was therefore cast down into the underworld, along with the 600 angels who were under his command, and together they helped Hades to punish sinners. The punishment, he revealed, involved putting wrongdoers into fire-filled pipes attached to swords projecting from huge wheels of fire, although quite how any distinction was made between those who had committed different sins is unclear. Following Hades' overthrow by Jesus, Satan and his cohorts, who were confined to hell, made use of certain 'swift ministers' or other devils that were allowed on to the surface of the earth, to tempt the living 'with sweetness of divers baits, that is by drunkenness and laughter, by backbiting, hypocrisy, pleasures, fornication' into sinning against God.

It is further related that after he had been told these things by Satan 'Bartholomew commanded him to go to hell', although we cannot help but wonder why he did not leave the

fallen first angel chained up where he was. The world would
have been a much better place had he done so, and the tourist
industry would have benefited enormously.

We also learn from the *Questions* that when Bartholomew
asked Jesus how many people in the world died each day,
Jesus replied that 30,000 did, although only 53 of them (or
0.17 per cent) were good enough to enter paradise. That was
in AD 33. If the same dismal proportion obtains today, then
out of the 500,000 or so people dying each year in Great
Britain (or 1370 a day) only two to three a day or 850 a year
will go to paradise.

The reports of NDEs which involved the wraiths of those
concerned travelling to the underworld are few and far
between in the immediate pre-Christian period. The Roman
writer Pliny does mention one incident in his *Natural
History*, however. The remarkable event happened during the
Sicilian War, a Roman civil conflict which pitted the forces of
Augustus Caesar against those of Sextus Pompey and his
brother Gneus, the sons of Pompey the Great, and which
lasted from 43 to 35 BC.

Pliny says that when Gabienus, Augustus' friend and
bravest naval commander, was taken prisoner by Sextus
Pompey, the latter brought him to shore and ordered his
throat to be cut. This was brutally done, and Gabienus was
left lying on the beach all day with his head almost cut off. But
then, as the evening drew in, he surprisingly recovered
consciousness and murmured to those standing around him
that he had a message for Pompey. Pliny says:

He begged the crowds of people who had assembled, that they
would prevail upon Pompey to come to him, or else send one of
his most influential friends, as he had just returned from the shades
below and had some important news to communicate. Pompey
accordingly sent several of his friends, to whom Gabienus stated
that the good cause and virtuous partisans of Pompey were well
pleasing to the infernal deities, and that the event would shortly
prove such as he wished: that he had been ordered to announce

to this effect, and that, as a proof of its truthfulness, he himself should expire the very moment he had fulfilled his commission; and his death actually did take place.

It is difficult to know what to make of this. How, we want to know, could the revived Gabienus possibly have spoken with a cut throat, for this would certainly have severed his trachea or windpipe? And even if he had managed to speak, would he really have told Pompey's friends that the 'infernal deities' considered Pompey's cause to be good and his followers virtuous? Yet Pliny took the trouble to mention the incident, which suggests that something odd happened. Gabienus may in fact have returned to life after having been left for dead on a beach, but if he had any message from the infernal deities, if we may so call them, it would have been that they were happy with Sextus Pompey for continuing the civil war, as this resulted in more wraiths descending to Hades. But their prediction that 'the event would shortly prove such as he wished' – if by 'he' Pompey is meant – was quite wrong: Pompey lost the struggle and, following his defeat in a naval battle, was forced to flee to Asia, where he was captured and killed by Mark Anthony.

As mentioned above, it is sometimes hazardous for a person to have the same name as someone whose fated moment of death has come. For it may mean that the angel or guide given the task of conducting the latter's wraith to the next world brings down the namesake by mistake, although this can presumably only occur if both are by chance simultaneously brought to the point of death.

In his *Dialogues*, St Gregory records the NDE of an 'honourable man' named Stephen, who personally related it to him. Stephen said that when he was away once on business in the city of Constantinople (modern Istanbul), he became seriously ill and died. His carers therefore sent for a surgeon to come and embalm him, so that his body could be sent home for burial. But there was a delay in finding one, and in the morning Stephen spontaneously revived. He recalled that while dead he was carried to hell, 'where he saw many things', which he had not believed in before. He then found himself taken to a place of judgement.

But when he was brought before the judge that sat there, he would not admit him to his presence, saying: 'I commanded not this man to be brought, but Stephen the smith': upon which words he was straightway restored to life, and Stephen the smith, that dwelled hard by, at that very hour departed this life: whose death did show that the words he heard were most true.

Even more astonishingly, when Stephen actually died some years later during a plague outbreak at Rome in AD 589, his death coincided with that of 'a certain soldier', who had known him but who, like Stephen before, shortly thereafter returned to life. The soldier said that when he died, he was suddenly brought to a bridge, although he did not know quite how, where he joined other wraiths, one of which was that of Stephen, waiting to cross it, and beyond which lay

. . . pleasant green meadows full of sweet flowers, in which also there were divers companies of men apparelled in white: and such a delicate savour there was, that the fragrant odour thereof did give wonderful content to all them that dwelt and walked in that place. Divers particular mansions also there were, all shining with brightness and light, and specially one magnifical and sumptuous house which was a building, the brick whereof seemed to be of gold, but whose it was, that he knew not.

But under that bridge ran a black, smoky, foul-smelling river, which bordered the paradise beyond. Those gathered with the soldier then attempted to cross the bridge, but not all made it over to the paradise on the other side, because the wicked were taken hold of and pulled into the water by black and ugly evil spirits that rose up from the river. One of these unfortunates was none other than Stephen, but before he could be pulled under the foul water, his arms were grasped by 'certain other white and beautiful persons', who suddenly appeared and attempted to haul him out. And thus a tug of war began, although the soldier did not see the final result owing to the fact that he revived and found himself back in his body. St Gregory explains this strange event by saying that Stephen had been a good Christian insofar as he frequently gave alms to the poor, but had trouble in resisting the sins of the flesh, which therefore prompted the struggle between the spirits of darkness and light in the next world.

The belief that hell lies underground and is reached by wraiths descending through volcanic vents and other earthly apertures is apparently confirmed by another incident related by St Gregory, which was told to him by Julian, a Church official and the son-in-law of the man to whom it happened.

In AD 526, the last year of the Ostrogoth king Theodoric the Great's rule at Rome, Julian reported that the ship taking his father-in-law from Sicily back to Rome suffered some damage in a storm and was obliged to cast anchor off the island of Liparis or Stromboli while repairs were done. He therefore took the opportunity, along with some of the other passengers, to land on the volcanic island and visit a solitary holy man who lived there. During their conversation, the hermit surprised them by asking if they had heard that Theodoric was dead, and when Julian's father-in-law protested that it could not be true, for he had left him alive at Rome, the hermit said there was no doubt about it, explaining: 'For yesterday at nine of the clock, he was without shoes or girdle, and his hands fast bound, brought betwixt John the Pope and Symmachus the Senator, and thrown into Vulcan's gulph, which is not far from this place.' And indeed, when the ship eventually returned to Rome, Julian's father-in-law learned that Theodoric had died on the same day (and at about the same hour) the hermit had seen him hurled into the fiery volcanic opening of Mount Stromboli.

The reason why Theodoric, whose reign had brought a long period of peace to Italy, was supposedly thrown into hell by those particular wraiths was that in addition to being a believer in the heretical Christian doctrine known as Arianism, which claimed that God and Jesus are not coeval – 'We are persecuted,' said its founder Arius, 'because we say that the Son has a beginning, but God is without beginning' – he was responsible for their deaths. He had Quintus Symmachus, the head of the Roman senate, executed in AD 525, and in 526 incarcerated Pope John I, who died in prison. Both men were thought to be traitors by Theodosius for favouring the reunification of the Eastern and Western Empires, although it seems evident from the fact that their wraiths hurled the king into Stromboli that they were innocent of the charge.

This was not the only occasion when a dead man's wraith was supposedly dispatched into hell via this volcano. Readers of my previous book *Disembodied Voices* will remember that I described the remarkable experience of a London merchant named Gresham who, while returning to London by ship from the Sicilian port of Palermo in about 1530, was blown off course and forced to take shelter on the lee side of Stromboli. He also took the opportunity to land on the island, and with eight crew members climbed to the summit of the volcano. While there, they suddenly heard a loud disembodied voice shout, 'Dispatch, dispatch, the rich Antonio is coming,' which caused them to flee in terror back to the shore and their ship. Later, on returning to Palermo, the winds still proving contrary, Gresham learned that Antonio the Rich, a well-known but corrupt Sicilian moneylender, had died on the same day the voice was heard, and at about the same time.

According to John Tregortha, author of *News From the Invisible World*, a similar event took place on the same volcanic island following the arrival there of four English ships on Friday, 15 May, the year probably being 1767. The next day the four captains, Edward Barnaby, William Bristow, Richard Brewer and Spinks, a passenger named Ball and several of the crew went ashore, the captains occupying themselves by shooting curlews. After having spent several hours so occupied, at about twenty minutes to four that afternoon, the captains called their men to them and prepared to return to their vessels. But just then, to their absolute astonishment, they all suddenly saw two men running with 'amazing swiftness' towards the cone of the volcano. Captain Spinks recorded:

Capt. Barnaby cried out, 'Lord, bless me! The foremost man is Mr Booty, my next neighbour in London.' He was in grey cloaths with cloth buttons. He that ran after him was in black. They both ran straight into the burning mountain, and at the instant was such a noise as made us all tremble. Capt. Barnaby said, 'I do not doubt, but it is old Booty running into hell:' and as soon as we came on board, he desired us to mark the time, and write it down in our Journals, which we did.

When the ships returned to Gravesend in October, and the captains gathered to congratulate themselves on their safe return, the wife of Captain Barnaby, who was at the dock to meet him, informed him that their elderly neighbour Booty had died, to which he replied, 'That we all know; for we saw him run into hell.' Mrs Barnaby laughingly repeated this odd tale to a friend, who in turn told Mrs Booty. So distressed was she by the claim that she sued Captain Barnaby for slandering her late husband. Yet when the case came to trial:

The four Captains, Mr Ball, and all the men made oath, that they saw him run very swiftly, and leap into the burning mountain: that he had on a grey coat with cloth buttons, (which was brought into the court, and exactly answered the description.) And that they all set it down just then in their Journals, which were also produced in Court, and answered the time when he died to two minutes, as appeared from the sexton of the Parish, and several others who were with him at his death.

It is difficult to know quite what to make of these accounts. Yet if they record actual events, then some wraiths at least are directed below ground after death, which likewise suggests that a subterranean enclosure is waiting to receive them. And because those so dispatched were sinners, the place, which is surely hot and fiery if its entrance is through volcanic cones, must be something like the interior of hell as described in the extracts above.

The above portrayals of hell together indicate that it does lie underground, that it is dark and hot, and that the wraiths of sinners are sent there to be punished in a variety of awful ways. Some of the accounts are certainly authentic, while others are by anonymous authors whose veracity is questionable. Did they make them up or did they base them, however loosely, on some unknown person's NDE? For despite there appearing to be a gradual development of the idea of hell, which seemingly evolved from a dark subterranean repository into a fiery torture chamber complete with Satan as overlord, whose horrors served the purpose of the Church by punishing errant Christians, we could equally well argue that hell was gradually revealed for what it is by respective visitants, notwithstanding the fact that their accounts were incorporated into Christian doctrine.

But if this horror is bad enough, the accounts of hell given by later and apparently genuine visitants are far worse. Indeed, it seems that hell is 'really hell'.

5

The Psychopompos

O love, love, hold me fast,
He draws me away from thee;
I cannot stem the blast,
Nor the cold strong sea:
Far away a light shines
Beyond the hills and pines;
It is lit for me.

From *The Hour and the Ghost*
by Christina Rossetti

The guide or *psychopompos* is a spirit or angel that conducts a
wraith into the next world. It is invariably reported to be
human in form, male in gender, and striking in appearance.
Strangely, female guides are rarely encountered. The guide
usually wears a simple gown, which is often of surpassing
whiteness and brilliance. His face, and sometimes his whole
body, emit a bright light. He usually speaks to the person he
is leading, but not always.

The ancient Greeks believed that all wraiths were led down
to Hades by the same deity, acting alone. This universal guide
was Hermes (or Mercury). Hermes was originally conceived
as being a bearded, middle-aged man, but by the fourth
century BC his image had become younger, handsomer and
clean-shaven. He was thought to wear winged sandals and a
distinctive conical hat with a brim, and to carry a *caduceus*, or
magic wand, with which he could induce both ordinary sleep
and entrancement. Hermes reputedly took wraiths below
ground via surface openings like caves and then to the under-

109

world through dark subterranean passageways, which implies that both he and his charges were quasi-physical.

But although afterlife guides are usually male, the pagan Teutons believed that the wraiths of warriors killed in battle or drowned at sea while on a raiding expedition were taken to the underworld by female spirits known as Valkyries (or 'choosers of the slain'). These were envisaged as being fierce-looking and mounted on horses. When the wraiths had been judged by the gods, those of noble birth who had died bravely were conducted by the Valkyries to Valhalla, where they were rewarded with wonderful feasts and drinking bouts and by re-enacting their past martial glories. As the handmaidens of Odin, the Valkyries were also thought to play an active part in warfare by boosting the courage and aggression of the combatants, inspiring the leadership of the kings, prompting assaults and rallies, and selecting those who were to die.

The chronicler Saxo Grammaticus (c.1140–1206) recounts how the Danish King Hadding (or Hading) was carried to the nether world by a woman. Apparently one winter's evening, when the king and his beloved Queen Ragnhild were dining together, there appeared in the hall before them a crone carrying some flowering stems of cowbane or water hemlock (*Cicuta virosa*). Startled by the sight of the blooms, King Hadding asked her where the plant grew at that time of year, whereupon, to everyone's astonishment, she threw her mantle over him and they vanished together into the underworld.

Such an instantaneous bodily transportation into the underworld could not really have occurred. Instead, as the woman's unannounced arrival suggests, the monarch had probably expressed an interest in experiencing the dissociative effects of cowbane, a poisonous plant with narcotic and hallucinogenic properties, and she had taken the opportunity to bring him some. She was therefore a wise-woman or witch, who knew not only where to find or how to grow cowbane, but also how to use it safely to enter the next world.

Following her directions, King Hadding would secretly have eaten just enough of the herb to put into him into a coma. She would have done the same, which enabled her to accompany him into the nether regions. Thus like Heracles before him, King Hadding used a dangerous narcotic plant to free himself from his physical body and to experience the wonder of death while still alive. Some commentators even believe that water hemlock, rather than its umbelliferous relative *Conium maculatum* or hemlock, was the source of the poisonous drink used to kill the Greek philosopher Socrates, but this seems unlikely in view of the fact that a fatal extract of cowbane causes muscle spasms, diarrhoea, convulsions and respiratory paralysis, which together result in a painful and rather pitiful death. Hence great skill and judgement is required to avoid these unpleasant symptoms and their fatal dénouement. Socrates' demise, by contrast, was completely painless.

The following is what Saxo Grammaticus says happened to King Hadding and his female companion when they vanished into the next realm, although in reality it would have taken place when they fell into a coma and left their bodies:

So they first pierced through a certain dark misty cloud, and then advancing along a path that was worn away with long thoroughfaring, they beheld certain men wearing rich robes, and nobles clad in purple; these passed, they at last approached sunny regions which produced the herbs the woman had brought away. Going further, they came on a swift and tumbling river of leaden waters, whirling down on its rapid current divers sorts of missiles, and likewise made passable by a bridge. When they had crossed this, they beheld two armies encountering one another with might and main.

It is evident that King Hadding was taken to Niflheim. To get there, he and the woman tramped along a road well worn by the many who had preceded them, passing various deceased members of the nobility (who had presumably died ordinary, non-heroic deaths) as they went, until they came to a sunny place where there was a river and a bridge. As I have noted,

111

the road, river and bridge are frequently encountered features of the next world. The growth there of 'herbs the woman had brought away' or water hemlock, indicates that the riverside region is somewhat like the Asphodel Fields of Greek myth, and thus lies between the bliss of Valhalla (or Elysium) and the punishment region of Nifel-hel (or Tartarus). The two armies fighting on the other side of the river consisted of the wraiths of slain warriors, some of whom would perhaps die again, and who would then be resurrected on the following day. But an obstacle lay ahead.

Then a wall hard to approach and to climb blocked their further advance. The woman tried to leap it, but in vain, being unable to do so even with her slender wrinkled body; then she wrung off the head of a cock which she chanced to be taking down with her, and flung it beyond the barrier of the walls; and forthwith the bird came to life again, and testified by a loud crow to its recovery of its breathing.

The arrival at a barrier like a wall, fence or river, beyond which it is forbidden or impossible for wraiths to go if they are to return to their bodies, has often been reported. In this respect it is pertinent to note that King Hadding did not try to climb the wall, which reveals that his trance or coma, while allowing the separation of his wraith, was non-fatal. However, the wise-woman, who evidently knew of the wall and the land of bliss lying beyond it, tried to prevent her return by climbing over it. Her failure indicates that her fated moment of death had not come. And because nobody could take a live cockerel down to the underworld, the story of the decapitated cock returning to life after being flung over the wall must symbolize Hadding's own recovery, for a cockerel is the king of his feathered domain. Cocks were once also sacrificed to the dead.

Hence the story of King Hadding's physical disappearance into the nether regions was the tactful or possibly Christian way to disguise the drug-induced near-death separation he

voluntarily underwent, which was too pagan or even demonic to be recorded as it happened.

Occasionally, the guide may be a deceased family member, loved one or friend, a former colleague, or even a well-known personage. Indeed, two or more such people sometimes form a welcoming party and may even come into the dying person's room to gather at his or her bedside. St Gregory records that when Bishop Probus of Reati lay dying, he insisted that his elderly father Maximus and the doctors he had summoned to care for him should go together to the dining room to eat their dinner, while leaving a boy with him in case of emergency. Then not long after they had left the room

. . . the little boy, standing by his bedside, suddenly saw certain men coming in to the man of God, apparelled in white stoles, whose faces were far more beautiful and bright than the whiteness of their garments: whereat being amazed and afraid, he began to cry out, and ask who they were: at which noise the Bishop also looking up, beheld them coming in and knew them, and thereupon comforted the little boy, bidding him not to cry, or be afraid, saying they were the holy martyrs St Juvenal and St Eleutherius that came to visit him.

The frightened boy, however, ran off to tell Maximus and the doctors what he had seen. They hurried back to the bedroom, only to find that Probus had died in the boy's absence and that the room was empty of the mysterious visitors. 'For those saints,' remarks Gregory, 'had carried his soul away in their company.'

In *A History of the English Church and People*, the Venerable Bede records the NDE of a man named Drycthelm of Cunningham, Northumberland, in AD 693. Drycthelm said that when he left his body, 'a handsome man in a shining robe was my guide, and we walked in silence in what appeared to be an easterly direction'. The guide first took him to a place of darkness and torment and then, on returning him to the light, brought him to 'a tremendous wall which seemed to be of infinite length and height in all directions' similar to the wall encountered by King Hadding. It had no windows or doorway, but none the less Drycthelm suddenly found himself standing on its top with his guide, from where he was able to look down at the pleasant, flowery scene within and upon its happy, white-robed inhabitants. The guide explained that they were blessed souls waiting to enter the kingdom of heaven.

A similar experience is described by Roger of Wendover (d. 1236) in the *Flowers of History*. In 1196, a monk at Evesham convent in Worcestershire, who had suffered a prolonged illness, collapsed and apparently died while abasing himself before a certain 'venerable man' he found sitting in the abbot's chair. The man, however, turned out to be an otherworldly guide, who was waiting for him to leave his body. The monk later said:

After he had raised me up, he took hold of my right hand firmly, yet gently, and we remained all the time with our hands linked together, and at that time I was deprived of all sense of body and mind. We then walked on a smooth road, straight towards the east, until we arrived in a large tract of country, dreadful to look at, in a marshy situation, and deformed with hard thickened mud.

While the monk of Evesham, like King Hadding, was led along a surface road or path, others have been taken into the sky. For example, Bede says that such an aerial adventure happened to St Fursey or Fursa (d. AD 648), an Irish-born monk who established a monastery at Burgh Castle in Norfolk. He later contracted a serious illness which brought him to the brink of death on two occasions, the first period of insensibility lasting for several hours, the second for three days. During both his wraith left his body and was carried upwards by three angels, although the second ascension was more dramatic, as Bede explains. 'When Fursey had been carried up to a great height, he was told by his angel guides to look back at the world. As he looked down, he saw what appeared to be a gloomy valley beneath him, and four fires in the air, not far from one another.'

The four fires, Fursey learned from the angels, were the sins of falsehood, covetousness, discord and injustice, which would one day consume the world and which actually merged together to form one vast fire as he watched. But while this seemed to be a vision, the fire's reality was attested by the fact that when the angels parted it to allow Fursey passage back to his body, some evil spirits who were burning the wraith of a sinner in its flames, pushed the man against Fursey as he passed, burning him on the jaw and shoulder. And then, after Fursey re-entered his physical self and recovered consciousness, he discovered that his flesh had acquired the burn mark inflicted on his wraith.

The appearance of injury marks on the body which reproduce those given to the wraith may sound impossible, but the phenomenon has often been reported. One interesting modern example is narrated by researchers Karlis Osis and Haraldson Erlender in their 1980 book *At the Hour of Death*, in which they compare the NDEs of Americans with those of Indians.

The incident can be better understood by noting, as the authors point out, that it is customary in India for a corpse to be bound to the stretcher on which it is carried to the funeral pyre. This helps explain the experience of the young Hindu girl in question who returned to life after being adjudged dead. She told the doctor who reported her experience that 'two messengers tied her with ropes on a stretcher and carried her up to God'. In the next world she saw many lovely women who were all cooking meals, and although she was tempted, like those taken to the fairy realm, to eat some of the food, she avoided doing so. This was perhaps fortunate for her as it seems that she had been transported aloft by mistake. Her doctor continued:

On a high place she saw a very influential person sitting in a decorated chair. He said to the messengers, 'Why did you bring her?' and then gave specifications of someone else who was to be brought. Those messengers then sent her back. She did not want to come back – the place was so beautiful. *Afterwards, signs of tying with ropes could be seen on her legs* [Author's italics].

It is difficult to understand why this reciprocal marking should occur, but the fact that the wraith itself can be marked or injured is further evidence that it is quasi-physical. In former times it was even believed that the wraith could be killed and that its demise resulted in the death of its physical self. But whether this led to the accompanying death of the person's consciousness is uncertain.

The double or wraith, as we have noted, may sometimes take the shape of an animal, and such a transfiguration gives us a possible explanation for werewolves. A person cannot physically change into a wolf, but it may be that while a suitable subject lies asleep or entranced, his or her double emerges in the guise of one. And if during its nocturnal rambles around the neighbourhood the werewolf was injured in any way, its wound would be reciprocally impressed on the person's physical form when the lupine doppelgänger returned to it. This is why those sleepers who give rise to a werewolf, which they may do without realising it, can often be identified by the injury they acquired from their transmogrified double.

Another celestial ascension happened to St Salvius or Sauve (*d.* AD 584), once Bishop of Albi (or Alby) in France, who clinically died after falling ill with a fever. Gregory of Tours (*c.* 540–590), writing in *The History of the Franks*, describes what happened next:

But at dawn, when all was made ready for the burying, the body stirred upon the bier. And, behold, colour came back to his cheeks; he roused himself as one startled from a deep sleep, and opening his eyes and lifting up his hands, he cried: 'O Lord of mercy, what hast Thou done to me, suffering me to return to this dark place of our earthly habitation, when it were better for me to know Thy compassion in heaven than the worthless life of this world.'

Such regret, and sometimes even anger, at being returned to one's body is commonly felt by those who are resuscitated, which perhaps suggests that doctors should not be over-zealous in bringing them back.

On being returned to his sick-bed, Salvius lay completely mute and uncommunicative for the next three days, apparently taking stock of what had happened to him. Then he broke his silence and told his brother monks how he had been conducted to heaven:

At the time when, four days ago, you saw me dead in my cell, I was carried away and taken to heaven by angels, from where it seemed to me that I had beneath my feet not only this muddy earth, but also the sun and the moon, the clouds and the stars; the angels led me through a doorway more brilliant than the day into a house filled by an ineffable light, wherein there was a floor resplendent with gold and silver; this was covered by so great a multitude, that one could not see across either the length or the breadth of the crowd.

In 1944 the Swiss psychoanalyst Carl Jung (1875–1961) was brought to the point of death by a heart attack. While lying unconscious he apparently left his body and, like St Salvius, was taken aloft and given a distant view of the earth and other astronomical bodies. He refers to the event as 'a vision' in his autobiography, but his description of it suggests that it was a genuine out-of-body experience:

It seemed to me that I was high up in space. Far below me I saw the globe of the earth, bathed in a gloriously blue light. I saw the deep blue sea and the continents. Far below my feet lay Ceylon, and in the distance ahead of me the subcontinent of India. My field of vision did not include the whole earth, but its global shape was plainly distinguishable and its outlines shone with a silvery gleam through that wonderful blue light . . . Later I discovered how high in space one would have to be to have so extensive a view – approximately a thousand miles!

Although Jung had neither angels to accompany him nor did he visit the marvellous celestial house shown to St Salvius, what happened next was equally remarkable. For when he turned to look towards the south, he noticed a huge block of dark stone floating near him in space. It had an entrance, beside which a dark-skinned Hindu wearing a white gown sat cross-legged. Jung went by the Hindu, who he knew was expecting him, and as he mounted the steps leading into the rock, he felt that 'everything I aimed at or wished for or thought, the whole phantasmagoria of earthly existence, fell away or was stripped from me', which initially caused him great pain. Yet the removal of these desires left Jung with a sense of being the sum of his life experiences and therefore complete. He realized there was nothing else he wanted or needed. 'I had everything that I was,' he noted, 'and that was everything.'

The stripping of ambition and desire from Jung's consciousness allowed him to see them for the ball and chains they really are, which in fact weigh down, impede and indeed entrap everyone. In this regard, we all make our own prisons. This perhaps explains why one of Fursey's angelic guides said to him, 'Every man's body is consumed by unlawful desire, and when death frees him from the body, he must make due atonement for his sins by fire.' Jung's revelation was also beautifully anticipated by Sir Henry Wotton (1568–1639) in the last verse of his poem entitled *The Character of a Happy Life*:

> This man is freed from servile bands
> Of hope to rise, or fear to fall;
> Lord of himself, though not of lands;
> And having nothing, yet hath all.

Going further into the rock, Jung approached a temple, where he intuitively comprehended there was a lighted room wherein waited all the people from his life on earth. He likewise realized that by joining them, he would at last discover his true place and meaning in the interlocking 'picture puzzle' of life, and know from where he had come and where he was going. But before he reached the temple, he was suddenly stopped in his tracks by the likeness of his doctor, who had come floating up from Europe to bar his way. Communicating with Jung telepathically, the physician informed him that he had been sent to tell him that 'I had no right to leave earth and must return. The moment I heard that, the vision ceased.' Indeed, the interruption coincided with his body's resuscitation by the doctor, which left Jung feeling furious at him for having deprived him of enlightenment – 'I felt violent resistance to my doctor because he had brought me back to life,' he comments, much like those returnees mentioned earlier.

A striking encounter with a guide happened to Jeremiah Carter, the vicar of Seathwaite, in north Lancashire. A contemporary chap-book relates that on Wednesday, 8 December 1630, when following the track over Warna Scar mountain towards the market town of Coniston, he suddenly became so 'heavisome' or tired that he was obliged to dismount from his horse. Having knelt to ask God for advice, he found he was unable to regain his feet and, while struggling to rise, lost consciousness and collapsed on the ground.

He lay where he had fallen for four days and nights, until he was found on Sunday, 12 December, by two of his parishioners. They carried him back to Seathwaite and to his desperately worried wife and children. Put to bed, the minister remained comatose for another six hours, but then suddenly regained his senses. After hurriedly composing his thoughts, he quietly revealed to those at his bedside that when he lay unconscious on the mountain, his wraith had been taken to the next world, although he then shocked them by adding that his return to life would be short, and was only granted to allow him to reveal what he had seen. This is what he said about his guide:

I was upon the aforesaid place, being the 8th of this Instant, there appeared to me one in bright Raiment, with a glorious Crown on his Head, whose Countenance shone more glorious than my Tongue or Pen can express; so that this poor Carcase began to shake and tremble. And he said to me, Fear not, for I am come to discover many strange and wonderful Things unto thee, that thou may'st cry aloud, and declare to the sinful Age their Sins and Transgressions. And behold the Angel of the Lord came and took me under the shadow of his wings: and mounted me up to the Heaven of Heavens.

Another wraith that was sent back 'as a messenger' belonged to the 16-year-old sister of James Turner of Carlton, Nottinghamshire, who collapsed and seemingly died on Tuesday, 16 November 1641, three days after her brother's wedding. However, when her mother, some twenty hours later, insisted on looking at her once more before she was nailed up in her coffin and buried, the girl 'even as one waking from a slumber raised up herselfe', much to her parent's astonishment and delight, and to the wonder of the burial party. It was soon noticed that she was far brighter and more cheerful than normal, even though she insisted that she would not be long with them. And on being asked by Mr Faber, the parson, where her soul had been while she lay dead, she replied:

I was overtaken neere the Bridge of the Brooke, by a comely old man, who saluted me saying, Daughter whither wilt thou, is thy father at home, I answered yea, then said he to me, come my loving Daughter, I must needs talk with thee, & tell thee that which is hidden from thee for great effect . . . So we came to a faire and costly Fort, no Princes Court like it, where we were let in, in which place we saw many bright Angels, shining like the Sun, all singing melodiously with cleare voices, *Holy, holy, holy, is our Lord God of Sabaoth.*

An elderly guide was also encountered by the nonconformist minister Dr Philip Doddridge (1702–51), when he left his body while asleep at a friend's house in London in 1725. The narrator of his strange experience, the Reverend Samuel

Clarke, the son of his best friend and a master at his school, says, 'He thought his soul left his body, and took its flight in some kind of fine vehicle, which though very different from the body it had just quitted, was still material.' This suggests of course that Dr Doddridge vacated his body in his double form. In this guise he travelled some distance from London.

He was met by one who told him he was sent to conduct him to the place appointed for his abode; from hence he concluded that it could be no other than an angel, though (as I remember) he appeared under the form of an elderly man. They went accordingly together till they came in sight of a spacious building, which had the air of a palace; upon enquiring what it was, his guide told him it was the place assigned for his residence at present.

While the 'spacious building' bears some resemblance to those seen by other visitors to the next world, it is pertinent to record that Dr Doddridge mused to his guide that God had promised his servants what had not been seen, heard, or conceived before, whereas he 'could easily have conceived an idea of such a building'. The guide, according to Dr Clarke, explained this anomaly in the following way: 'The scene first presented was contrived on purpose, to bear a near resemblance of those he had been accustomed to on earth, that his mind might be more easily and gradually prepared for those glories that would open upon him in eternity; and which would at first have quite dazzled and overpowered him.'

If we can accept Dr Doddridge's experience as being something more than a dream, it reveals that the buildings and landscapes initially encountered in the next world have no objective existence, but are instead specially created phantoms which help wraiths adjust to their new existence and thus prepare them for the glorious reality they will eventually experience.

Each otherworldly landscape or scene thus mimics the function of the wraith itself, which is to provide the separated consciousness with a familiar environment, thereby enabling it to cope with the loss of its physical self. This is why 'life' in the next world, to begin with at least, resembles life here, with people not only looking the same but interacting with each other as they do now, although the surroundings for the good are far brighter and more pleasant than they are for the bad.

But not all guides conduct the wraiths around a landscape. Some instead give moral guidance or advice, helping them to decide whether they should remain where they are, which most would prefer to do, or return to their bodies. This often happens when those concerned have dependants like children, or whose lives have been spent selfishly and materialistically. An example of the latter type is London psychotherapist Maureen Grey, who before she began her career had thoughtlessly followed the carefree, self-indulgent upper-class social round. But in 1977, at the age of fifty-two and while travelling in India, she was struck down with a serious febrile illness, which brought her to the brink of death. Then one day she suddenly found herself floating outside her body, up near the room's ceiling. From that position, she noted, her physical self looked like 'a shabby old coat that needed to be thrown away. It was just a body, not me.'

Going higher, Maureen passed through the ceiling and entered a total blackness, into which she apparently began falling. It was in this strange situation that she met her guide or adviser. 'I became aware of a man wearing a long white robe, with sandals on his feet. There was a wonderful light behind him, so his face was in shadow, but I could still see that he had the most beautiful blue-grey eyes and a brown skin. I'd have said he was Eastern rather than Western.' The man exuded such a profound love that Maureen threw herself into his arms, and she thereupon understood that he knew all about her, not least the problems and difficulties which had prompted her to behave as she had. He told her she had to make the following choice: 'I could move on or go back,' she said, 'but what mattered were not material considerations but my spiritual development. He indicated that if I went back, things wouldn't be easy, but my life would change radically.'

Maureen opted for returning to the world, and not long afterwards she found herself back in her body. This marked the start of her return to first physical, and then mental, health, for when she went back to England she discovered that the shallowness and frippery of her former existence no longer had any appeal for her. Then, to her complete surprise, she was given the opportunity to read psychology at an American university. She took up the challenge, worked hard and eventually gained a degree, and afterwards went on to became a practising psychotherapist. She has since spent her time helping others, and has been spiritually transformed as a result.

An interesting encounter with a guide was related by a young woman named Mary Stone, who was born in 1741. She was a farmer's daughter of Wateringbury, in Yalding parish, Kent, and was known as 'the Kentish wonder'. She became ill with the ague (or malaria) on Sunday, 7 August 1757, languished feverishly for the next seven weeks and seemingly vacated this world for the next on 22 September. Her parents, John and Mary Stone, were devastated by her loss and postponed the funeral for four days. Yet like Mistress Turner of Carlton, Mary Stone also returned unexpectedly to life. This happened when her mother gave her a farewell kiss as she lay in her coffin. She was quickly removed from it and warmed in front of a fire, and then put to bed for the night. She slept well, and awoke the following morning feeling entirely normal.

When Mary was visited by her minister, Dr John Cook, and his curate later that day, she gave them this account of what had first happened to her while she lay dead:

When my spirit wandered from my body, I met with a man all in white raiment, which proved my guide; and he said, Follow me, and no harm shall come unto you; and so I followed him. We first walked along very pleasant green fields, where was a great many spirits wandering to and fro, some of whom I knew when alive; and there we walked a day or more.

From this delightful spot, the guide conducted Mary to within sight of hell, which frightened her greatly, and from there, after a further walk of 'a day or two more', to the celestial Jerusalem, replete with golden walls, just as it was shown to the fictional Paul by his angelic escort. Mary hoped she might be allowed to stay there, but was disappointed to learn that she had to return to her body, although the guide did make two prophecies of interest to her, one of which concerned her longevity and future heavenly prospects:

I asked him concerning the great and mortal sickness, which now is so fatal in England. He said it would be pretty well over in three months, and that this year would be a plentiful year, and the greatest part of it very healthful. He bid me lead a sober godly life, and in five and twenty years I should come to that celestial place. He bid me exhort all Christian people to repent their sins, and lead a godly life, and the sickness would soon abate among them; and that, within these three months, grim Death with his cruel dart would sweep away a great many of this land.

Such prophecies of the future were once quite frequently made by guides encountered during an NDE. For example, when the disembodied Mistress Turner became 'very pensive' at the prospect of having to return to her body, the 'comely old man' who escorted her told her to 'rest contented, for the short time shall quickly have an end, and within 5 dayes thou shalt be brought again to this place', which proved entirely accurate, as on the fifth day after her revival the young woman lay down on her bed, prayed for fifteen minutes with those with her, and then 'to all their thinking she fell asleepe, and never after stirred but dyed'.

Likewise, the angelic guide of Jeremiah Carter gave him a dire prophecy of coming mishaps. 'There will be a great Damage by Hail, Thunder and Lightnings in several Places this Year, Raging Fevers, Small-Pox, and other Distempers, which will come upon many unawares, and tumble their Bodies to the Grave, so that there will be a Sweep in this land, that the Inhabitants may learn

Righteousness.' If we remember that 'this Year' applies to the year from 12 December 1630, in other words to 1631, then the prophecy regarding sickness hurrying many unexpectedly to the grave is accurate, as there was a bad outbreak of bubonic plague that year. We also know from the diaries of John Evelyn that there was 'an extraordinary dearth' of corn in England in 1631, which made its price shoot up and which led to widespread hunger and starvation. And while I have been unable to discover if 1631 had more hailstorms and smallpox outbreaks than normal, the two problems I have mentioned indicate that the year was generally difficult for most people.

A case reported by the Reverend David Simpson, which was told to him by the men concerned, is sufficiently unusual to be included here. He does not say when exactly it occurred, but it probably took place in the second half of the eighteenth century. One of the men, a deckhand, suffered a sudden collapse when he tried to row ashore from a trading vessel owned by Thomas Clarke and his brother, which had been prevented from sailing from the Isle of Man by unfavourable winds. The brothers, both Methodists, hauled the unconscious sailor back on board and with some difficulty managed to revive him. He was then put into a bunk and well tended until he recovered sufficiently to speak. And what he then disclosed was startling.

I have been out of the body, and have seen wonderful things. As soon as I jumped into the boat my spirit departed, and I found myself in the custody of two devils, in the shape of black bears, who dragged me to a lime kiln, out of which I saw flames of fire ascending. I shrieked horribly, and just as they were going to throw me in, an angel dressed in white robes, whose face resembled Mr Mason's, the Methodist preacher, suddenly appeared, and said to the devils, He is not yours, let him go; upon which, they immediately vanished.

The white-robed angel then became the sailor's guide, and led him away from the awful lime kiln and towards a more salu-

125

brious environment, whose scenes are described in the next chapter. And happily, even though he believed he was destined soon to die, the man not only made a full recovery but, having witnessed the flames into which he was about to be thrown, changed his whole way of life in order hopefully to avoid them when his end came.

These early NDEs differ from many modern ones in lacking the now-familiar journey down a dark tunnel and the emergence into a bright and intelligent light at its end, which converses directly with the wraith concerned. Indeed, most involve the straightforward separation of the wraith from its physical self and its subsequent meeting with the guide at a place nearby – Mistress Turner's guide, for example, was waiting for her by a local bridge – or sometimes its translocation directly into the next realm of being, where a waiting guide then shows it the sights.

Many modern wraiths are also shown a 'life review', which consists of a series of colourful replays of all or parts of their lives, and which, with a simultaneously acquired heightened sensitivity, enables them to evaluate their existence. In this way a personal judgement is reached, and indeed most people find themselves wanting. Not only do they recognize their own selfishness, but they feel deep shame at their failure to do anything with their life that was worthwhile.

Some early NDEs did include a life review, although this was usually presented in the form of either a spoken or a written revelation, rather than a pictorial playback. We have already noted that the *Apocalypse of Paul* says each person's good deeds and sins are supposedly reported to God twice a day by his or her guardian angel. The latter also wrote them down, thereafter keeping the daily notes as a permanent *aide-mémoire*. 'Paul' describes how the guardian angel of one wraith, who had lied about its sins, was summoned into God's presence. 'And the angel of the sinful soul came, having a writing in his hands, and said: These, Lord, that are in mine hands, are all the sins of this soul from its youth up unto this day.'

How such testimony was revealed during an NDE (or indeed at death) apparently depended on the person's level of literacy. The wraiths of the illiterate were verbally addressed by their guide or guardian angel, whereas those who could read were generally shown a written account of their good and bad deeds. One early example of the latter type is recorded by the Venerable Bede, to whom it was told by a Northumbrian bishop named Pecthelm, and actually took place before the man in question had died.

The man, who was a military commander of Ceolred, king of Mercia (ruled 704–9), was entirely honest and capable in his professional life, but was guilty of private laxity. Yet he refused either to change his ways or confess his sins, despite being frequently urged to do so by the pious monarch. And when he fell sick with a painful illness, he would still not confess and ask for forgiveness, saying that if he did so when ill, he would be accused of acting solely out of fear. He would therefore, he said, wait until he regained his health.

However, his sickness worsened, and King Ceolred, worried that he might die and so lose his soul, again visited him and begged him to recant and confess. But the soldier, grimacing through his pain, told the king it was too late, for he had had 'the knowledge of my wickedness set clearly before my eyes'. And he explained that not long before two very handsome young men clad in shining white robes had come and sat down with him, one at the head, the other at the foot of the bed. 'One of them produced a tiny but very beautiful book, and gave it to me to read. When I looked at it, I found all the good deeds that I had ever done recorded, but they were few and trifling. Then they took back the book, but said nothing to me.'

These angelic figures were then joined by numerous wicked spirits or demons, dark in colour and very ugly, who seemed to fill up the entire house. Their chief brought a huge 'horrible-looking' and heavy book into the dying man's room, which was likewise given to him to read.

When I read it, I found all my crimes clearly recorded there in black letters, not only my sins of act and word, but even of the least thought. And he [the chief demon] said to the glorious white robed men who were sitting beside me: 'Why are you sitting here? You know very well that this man belongs to us.' They replied: 'You are right. Take him, and enrol him in your company of the damned.'

The white-robed men then disappeared, and two of the demons struck the invalid with their tridents, one on his head, the other on his feet, inflicting great pain, which slowly moved towards his middle. When the pains met and united, the man died in despair, knowing that he would be straight-way 'dragged down through the gates of Hell'.

The experience of the Reverend Henry Watts is a later example. He reputedly died from an acute fever at about eight o'clock in the evening of Friday, 5 August 1698. His family resolved to bury him quickly, as was usual in the summer when bodies soon began to putrefy and smell, and opted for that Sunday. A colleague from a neighbouring parish came to conduct his funeral service. But when in due course he led the cortège to the graveside, 'a noise of Groaning and Struggling in the coffin was heard just as they were putting it into the Grave', which shocked and frightened everybody. The burial proceedings were immediately halted and the coffin quickly opened, whereupon its occupant, by raising his hand and mumbling a few words, revealed to the startled onlookers that he was still very much alive. Taken home and put into a warm bed, the revived minister, though trembling and weak, insisted on telling those gathered around what had happened to him while he was dead. He said:

As soon as my Soul was separated from this lump of Earth, all my Sins were exposed before me, seemingly Engraven as on a Marble Table in Crimson Letters, which very much astonished me, the Scroll was so large every tittle of them being fresh in my Memory, which caused me almost to dispare, when at that very instant my good Angel presented me with a White and Pleasant Rool, in which my good Acts were Written in Letters of Shining Gold, as also my Holy Prayers, and Charitable Practices, which shin'd above all the rest more gloriously; so that a great and Heavenly Joy seiz'd my Soul; so waiting and expecting my Sentence I suddainly was bid to return again to the Body I had left, in order to warn and perswaid Presumptious Sinners to forsake their Sins, and put on the happy and white Rayment of Christ Jesus. But Oh my Friends, I cannot express the bitter Loathing and Hateful difficulties, with which I re-entered this so foul and Abominable Carcass.

That was not the entirety of Henry Watts' out-of-body experience; he was also shown the wrongdoings of his sister along with his own. This came to light when she quite reasonably asked him if he could provide 'any certain Testimony for human Satisfaction, of his being in another World', whereupon he privately told her of the 'many Secret Sins' she had committed. The unexpected disclosure shocked her so much that she wept bitter tears, although quite what those sins were remains a mystery.

The only problem with the Henry Watts story is that I have discovered three separate accounts of it, which relate essentially the same tale, but variously make him the vicar of Ripley in Yorkshire, St Clements in Oxford, and Reigate in Surrey. My research, however, has shown that none of these places had a Henry Watts for their vicar, in 1698 or at any other time. So it is impossible to know if the event happened as described or if it is an early example of an urban myth. I would therefore be delighted to hear from any reader who knows of an actual seventeenth century Reverend Henry Watts.

In later times even the very literate were shown pictorial representations of their life, one interesting example of which was seen by Dr Philip Doddridge, whom I have already mentioned. After he had been taken to the 'spacious building', he was led 'through a kind of saloon into the inner parlour', where a golden cup embossed with a vine and a cluster of grapes stood upon a table. When he asked about the meaning of the cup, he was told by his angelic guide that 'it was the cup in which the Saviour drank new wine with his disciples in his Kingdom'. Not long afterwards Jesus himself came into the room (although no description of him is given), and when he had raised the genuflecting Dr Doddridge from his knees, Jesus insisted that the doctor should share the wine with him in the manner indicated by the angel. Following this incredible intimate meeting, Dr Doddridge discovered the review of his life.

As soon as his Lord had retired, and his mind was a little composed, he observed the room was hung round with pictures, and upon examining them more attentively, he discovered, to his great surprise, that they contained the history of his own life. The most remarkable scenes he had passed through, being there represented in a most lively manner. It may easily be imagined how much this would affect his mind; the many temptations and trials he had been exposed to, and the signal instances of the divine goodness towards him in the different periods of his life, which by this means were all presented at once to his view, excited the strongest emotions of gratitude.

Dr Doddridge's strong emotions in fact woke him up, and so impressive and real was the experience to him that for a long time afterwards 'tears of joy flowed down his cheeks'.

In former times wraiths were often shown both the delights of heaven and the torments of hell by their guides – as indeed they sometimes still are – and the contrast between the two naturally sharpened the piquancy. Such direct evidence of beauty and peace on the one hand, and pain and horror on the other, was naturally upsetting and life-changing, for the choice was stark, and prompted the returnees to spend the rest of their lives praying and doing good. And as an additional safeguard, the guide himself sometimes advised the soon-to-be-returned wraith, as happened to Mary Stone, to lead a godly and sober life and thereby to avoid the fires of hell.

One interesting case of observation followed by self-insight and personal transformation is reported by John Tregortha. It happened in the mid-eighteenth century and involved a young man from Crewkerne, Somerset, named Henry Webb, who though born to respectable parents, grew into a wild, lazy and intractable youth. He ran away from both his master (he was apprenticed to a shoemaker) and his parents, and fell in with bad company and quickly 'became a reprobate liver, a common swearer, and sabbath-breaker, having no thought of goodness or religion at all'.

Henry's problems were made more intractable by the fact that he refused to acknowledge that his behaviour was in any way wrong or immoral, a characteristic which he shares with many modern hooligans. He thus spent his time in a moral vacuum, and took advantage of every opportunity that came his way to misbehave, shirk, lie, cheat and generally be obnoxious.

The scales fell from his eyes in 1750, at age twenty, however, when a severe loss of blood following a blood-letting operation brought him to the brink of death. What Henry saw during his NDE is described in the next two chapters. Here it is sufficient to say that, upon leaving his body and entering the next realm, he was refused admittance into heaven by those manning its gate, a rejection which stunned him and which was followed by a visual recollection of his sins.

It was at this moment he first had any sense of his sinful life; for as quick as fire catches the dry stubble, so quick and penetrating were the words of the shining one; for no sooner were they spoke, than all the sins he had ever committed in his life seemed to rise before him with all their weight and horror, so that he believes the agonies of hell itself cannot exceed what he felt at that time.

Henry was next given a view into hell and saw the terrible fate which had befallen several of his former friends, and which, he realized, now awaited him – unless he could make amends for his sins by turning over a new leaf. His anxieties were made

131

even worse by the fact that a fortnight after he had been resuscitated, he developed a serious fever which seemed likely to finish him off, and during which he begged all his visitors 'to pray with him and for him'. But he survived this illness and in due course returned to his former occupation, although he was a completely changed man.

He has ever since lived a regular, sober, christian life shunning all loose and unprofitable company, not being able to hear any prophane discourse or oaths from the mouths of others, without the greatest uneasiness, and even reproving them for it; he daily bewails his former course of life, and frequently applies to God in prayer, being never so easy as when he is engaged in some religious duty or conversation.

These accounts show that we have lost not only the single guide in the form of a divinity like Hermes, which is perhaps not surprising, but also the personal guide in the guise of our own guardian angel, which is more puzzling because if guardian angels exist it would seem that they are ideally placed to perform this function. Yet surprisingly neither Plato nor the author of the *Apocalypse of Paul* give them such a role. The latter work in fact portrays them as nothing other than angelic snoopers, busily jotting down what each of us does and telling tales to God *twice every day!* But it does provide the first description of the guides that take wraiths into God's presence after bodily death, one type being 'the compassionate angels' who lead the good, the other 'the unmerciful angels' who conduct the bad. The former have faces that shine like the sun, which is a feature that has been reported by some NDE returnees who have been met by guides, although these have not taken them into God's presence.

We can therefore conclude that the guides who meet those who have an NDE are completely unknown to them and never claim any personal relationship with them. The guide is always male and is usually clad in a long shining white robe, although occasionally, as we shall see in the next chapter, it is

132

black. And while the guide may be young and handsome, he is just as likely to be elderly, although pleasant or even striking to look at. His main function is to show the wraith the sights of heaven and hell, which is done as a corrective measure, for the consequences of further sinfulness are made plain, although the choice (if there is one) about whether or not the wraith should to return to the physical body is generally left open.

6

Gardens and Green Fields

The fields are green, the plants do thrive,
  The streams with honey flow.
From spices, odours and from gums
  Most precious liquor, grow,
Fruits hang upon whole woods of trees,
  And they shall still do so.
        From *A Hymn of Paradise*, author unknown

One commonly reported feature of an NDE, which is experienced in about a quarter of cases, is for the subjects to find themselves walking through a pastoral landscape of green fields or meadows. These may also border or contain a flower-filled garden or gardens. Both fields and gardens have a beauty which far surpasses that of their earthly counterparts; their colours, for example, are brighter and more vivid. Indeed, so exquisite are they that many believe themselves to be in heaven, although it also contains an inner region, whose magnificence and glory, as one returnee put it, 'made every thing else that had pass'd for wonderful before, to look mean, and sordid'.

We have already noted that green fields and gardens comprised a distinct part of the pagan nether world, and were thought to exist either in the subterranean regions or somewhere upon the earth's surface, usually in the far west. The widely held belief in their existence was doubtlessly based on the experiences of people who had returned from apparent death caused by illness or injury, or who had deliberately induced such a state by ingesting controlled amounts of plant poisons.

The name 'paradise', which as we have seen is derived from the Old Persian word for a park or garden, is often given to such a divine panorama, and paradise in the form of the Elysian Fields was the final (and longed for) destination of good and worthy pagan Greeks, as it is for modern Muslims. But if we accept the description of the third heaven by the author of the *Apocalypse of Paul*, paradise encircles the celestial Jerusalem or the city of Christ, which is the desired destination of Christians. The city of Christ and its encircling gardens, fields and rivers resemble in general form the typical layout of Near Eastern gardens like that constructed by the Persian King Cyrus at Sardis in Lydia, in about 548 BC. These often had a magnificent walled inner palace or sanctum, wherein the king or emperor stayed with his family and invited guests, who found in its shaded circumambulatory pathways beauty to the eye and relief from the barren and burning desert around.

The concept of a celestial paradise is so seductive to Muslims, that in the Middle Ages, according to Marco Polo, an eastern king named Alaodin of Mulehet, counterfeited one replete with skilled musicians and willing virgins. Then he drugged young warriors and took them to the bogus paradise, and after having allowed them to savour fully its sensorial delights, rendered them insensible again and had them returned to the ordinary world, into which they woke with bitter disappointment and regret. Alaodin next sent them out to assassinate his enemies, missions which would certainly result in their own deaths. But having, as they thought, sampled the divine reward that awaited them, they went out with all the fanaticism of a modern Islamic fundamentalist. *Plus ça change, plus c'est la même chose!*

In William Shakespeare's *Henry V*, the hostess or landlady of a tavern in Eastcheap describes the death throes of Falstaff, the Bard's great comic character, in the following way:

'. . . a' parted even just between twelve and one, even at the turning o' the tide: for after I saw him fumble with the sheets and play with flowers and smile upon his fingers' ends, I knew there was but one way; for his nose was as sharp as a pen, and a' babbled of green fields.'

Thus Falstaff's apparently random fumblings, the change in the shape of his nose and the fact that he 'babbled of green fields', were indicators of his imminent demise. Later in the same speech, the good woman adds:

'So a' bade me lay more clothes on his feet: I put my hand into the bed and felt them, and they were as cold as any stone: then I felt to his knees, and so upward, and all was as cold as any stone.'

Shakespeare's reference to the seeing of green fields by the dying (and also, for that matter, by those who have returned from the dead) indicates that the phenomenon was common knowledge in 1599, when the play was written.

A remarkably similar description of the signs of death is found in *The History of Life and Death*, written by Francis Bacon (1561-1626) and published in 1623. Indeed, their similarity suggests that Bacon, a contemporary of Shakespeare (1564-1613), may have plagiarized *Henry V*. If so, it would have been entirely in keeping with the character of the man, for Bacon, notwithstanding his interest in science and his belief in the superiority of experiment over theory, often built upon the ideas of others, excusing himself by saying, 'I am glad to do the part of a good househen, which without any strangeness will sit upon pheasants' eggs.' The relevant portions of Bacon's account read:

The immediate proceeding signs of Death are, great unquietness and tossing in the bed, fumbling with the hands, catching and grasping hard, gnashing with the teeth, speaking hollow, trembling of the neather lip, paleness of the face . . . changing of the whole visage (as the nose sharp, eyes hollow, cheeks fallen), contraction and doubling of the coldness in the extreme parts of the body, in some, shedding of blood or sperm, breathing thick and short, falling of the neather chap, and such like.

Alternatively, the similarity of the passages may support the view that Francis Bacon was the real author of at least some of the plays ascribed to Shakespeare, which would mean that the hostess's description of the signs preceding Falstaff's death came from his own observations made at the bedsides of the dying. But the main interest of *The History of Life and Death* to us occurs a few pages later, when Bacon describes an experiment performed by 'a certain *Gentleman*', who wished to know what it was like to be hanged. The rash young man, having elevated himself by standing on a stool, placed his head in the noose of a rope tied to a ceiling beam, and then swung himself into space. His hopes of being easily able to remount the stool, and thereby relieve the pressure on his neck proved ill-founded, and he was only saved from strangulation by the friend who attended him.

He was asked afterwards what he felt. He said he felt no pain, but first he thought he saw before his eyes a great fire and burning; then he thought he saw all black and dark; lastly it turned to a pale blew, or sea-water green; which colour is also often seen by them which fall into *swoonings*.

These visual impressions are significant because they appear to be precursors of the scenes often reported by those who say they have witnessed both the fire and darkness of hell and beautiful green fields. However, we must remember that Bacon is not giving the young man's own account of what he saw, but rather another person's, which may or may not be accurate.

A similar experiment was supposedly carried out in 1868 by another anonymous English gentleman, who published an account of it in a work entitled *Studies in Biology*. The man, to the horror and consternation of his wife and daughter, first built a gallows in his garden, which prompted his daughter, who considered the venture an 'exhibition of crazy eccentricity', to threaten to run off with the butler unless he desisted. But her father, who was acting, as he claimed, in 'the pursuit of science and the elucidation of truth', countered her threat by sacking the butler and by locking her in the cellar.

At noon on the appointed day, assisted by Tony, his foot-man, the man mounted the gallows, put the noose over his head and stepped into space. He immediately regretted having done so, but was unable to communicate this to Tony, for he had omitted to put a white silk handkerchief in the breast pocket of his dinner jacket, whose removal was to be the signal for Tony to cut the rope. But the footman, acting with commendable rapidity and independence, cut the rope anyway, and thereby saved the life of his foolhardy employer. When the man eventually came to his senses, he wrote the following somewhat familiar and oddly poignant description of what he had seen in the beyond. It does not include any mention of green fields, however:

Every sin of mine – of thought, word, and deed, blazed before me in characters of fire, and from amid the lurid blazonry, the meek, calm face of my mother, who had been thirty years in the grave, looked upon me with unutterable tenderness and love. Then the earth gave way, and I was hurled down headlong into the unfath-omable darkness. In my descent I was dashed against revolving and tremendous worlds, with rivers of blood rolling into oceans of fire . . . I became unconscious of my material identity, and had only a mysterious existence as a spirit of suffering infused through a thousand worlds . . . The amalgamated worlds became identi-fied with my brain. Then ten thousand gigantic forms of shadow shot through it arrows of red fire . . . Then it seemed that after the lapse of many thousand years all the thunderpeals since the creation of the world combined in one tremendous roar, the skull of my tortured brain was split, and the boundless world-shadow of agony rolled down – down into vacuity and nothingness!

When John Smith, the errant son of a Yorkshire farmer, was hanged for burglary and felony at Tyburn on Wednesday, 12 December 1705, he was saved from death by the arrival of a messenger bearing a reprieve. Smith was immediately cut down and carried to a nearby house, where efforts were successfully made to revive him. But while he did report experiencing 'a great pain' when he was first swung into space, this not only soon ended but was ironically less than the pain he felt when he was being resuscitated. His sole visual impression when he was turned off resembles that seen by Bacon's 'certain *Gentleman*': 'I felt my spirits in a strange commotion, violently pressing upwards, which, having forced their way to my head, I, as it were, saw a great blaze of glaring light, which seemed to go out at my eyes with a flash, and then I lost all sense of pain.'

Readers of *Buried Alive* will remember the case of Anne Green, who was hanged at Oxford on Saturday, 14 December 1650, for having supposedly aborted her bastard child. No reprieve interrupted her half-hour suspension, and upon being cut down from the gallows she was taken away to be dissected. But before the surgeons could get to work with their scalpels, Anne showed signs of life and was forthwith fully restored by the medical men.

Richard Watkins, the author of an account of her trial and execution entitled *Newes from the Dead* (1651), states that he can give no report of 'what visions this maid saw in the other world; what cœlestiall musicke, or hellish howling she heard; what spirits she conversed with, and what Revelations she brought backe with her, concerning the Present Times, or the events of things to come', as she remembered nothing of the experience. Her absence of recollection, however, is disputed by Robert Plot in *The Natural History of Oxfordshire* (1705). It seems Plot had access to the account of Anne's revival penned by Dr (later Sir) William Petty (1623–87), one of the surgeons who helped resuscitate her. Petty, like many modern doctors and scientists, was dismissive of supposed memories of the next world, yet he apparently did learn something of what Anne had seen from her excited female visitors.

After some time Dr Petty hearing she had discoursed with those about her, and suspecting that the Women might suggest unto her

to relate something of strange Visions and Apparitions she had
seen, during the time she seemed to be Dead (which they already
had begun to do, telling about that she said, she had been in a
fine Green Meadow, having a River running round it, and that all
things there glittered like Silver and Gold) he caused all to depart
the Room.

In *Buried Alive* I also described the post-gallows recovery
of William Duell. He was hanged on Monday, 24 November
1740, for the robbery, rape and murder of a young woman in
Acton, but revived while being washed in preparation for the
dissectors. Writing in *Tyburn Tree: Its History and Annals*,
Alfred Marks says that 'Duel(l) or Dewell did not recollect
being hanged: he said that he had been in a dream; that he
dreamed of Paradise, where an angel told him his sins were
forgiven.' But clearly, if Duell 'dreamed' he was in paradise, it
probably means he found himself in either a beautiful garden
or a green field. There was a similar recovery from hanging in
1782, although the details of the event have proved impossible
to find. Marks only notes that the felon concerned was named
John Hayes, who recalled having been in 'a beautiful green
field' when he came back to life.

In the last chapter we considered Roger of Wendover's
account of the NDE of the monk of Evesham, whom we left
being led along an otherworldly road by his guide. This
byway first took them past hell, where the monk saw the
dreadful punishments inflicted on the evil and ungodly. But
further on they came to a far more pleasant area, a grassy and
flowery plain similar to that visited by Er, which was the first
resting place of those who had suffered in hell and were now
finding respite and consolation. As we would expect, the
region was populated by vast numbers of wraiths.

The light began by degrees to appear more pleasant; here the
fragrance of a sweet odour, there the richness of a plain flourish-
ing with many kinds of flowers afforded us incredible pleasure. In
this plain we found endless thousands of men or spirits who, after

passing through their punishments, were enjoying the happy rest of the blessed. Those whom we found in the first portion of this plain, had garments white indeed, but not shining, but there did not appear any blackness or stain in them, although they shone in an inferior degrees of whiteness.

I have also mentioned earlier the post-mortem experience of the sixth-century soldier reported by St Gregory, whose 'soul was in such sort carried out of his body' and who suddenly found himself standing with many others by a bridge over a very black and noxious-smelling river, on the far side of which, however, were 'pleasant green meadows full of sweet flowers, in which also there were divers companies of men apparelled in white', which closely resembled the scene witnessed above by the monk of Evesham. But among the crowd waiting to cross the bridge were wicked wraiths, who did not make it over. They either 'fell into that dark and stinking river' or were pulled in by evil spirits who rose from it and took hold of them, whereas 'those that were just and not hindered by sin, securely and easily passed over to those pleasant and delicate places'.

People recovering from an NDE frequently report that a river forms the border between this world and the next, although it is seldom as unpleasant as that seen by Gregory's soldier. Alternatively, a fence, a wall or some other barrier is encountered. If a bridge gives access to beautiful paradisial meadows on the river's far side, visitants are given to understand that if they cross the bridge, then they cannot return to their bodies. And whereas most of those whose bodies are still capable of being resuscitated want to cross the bridge and thus bid a permanent farewell to their physical self, they usually choose to return if they have some pressing reason for so doing, such as young children or elderly parents to care for – or they may want to take the opportunity to make amends for a life lived selfishly or criminally.

A typical river and bridge scene was reputedly witnessed by a Franciscan monk – 'a man of Singular holiness' – who

lived at a convent in Tübingen, Germany, on the morning of
Monday, 30 June 1522. After celebrating matins, the monk
returned to his cell, lay on his bed, fell into a deep sleep – and
suddenly found himself standing at the border of the next
world! According to Desiderius Erasmus (1466–1536), the
monk claimed:

Methought I was standing by a little Bridge that led into a
Meadow, so wonderfully fine, what with the Emerald Verdue, and
freshness of the Trees and Grass; the infinite Beauty, and Variety of
Flowers, and the fragrancy of all together that all the Fields on this
side of the River lookt dead, blasted, and withered, in Comparison.

Moments later, to the monk's surprise, a good friend of his,
the well-known humanist and Hebraist Johann Reuchlin
(1455–1522), passed by him, saying a blessing in Hebrew as he
went, and walked on to the bridge. He was half across it when
the monk, coming to himself, began to follow him over, but
'he lookt back and bade me stand off. Your time (says he) is
not yet come: but five years hence you are to follow me. In the
mean while, be you a Witness, and a Spectator, of what's
done.'
  On gaining the far side, Reuchlin was joyfully greeted by
none other than St Jerome, who was clad in a long gown 'as
Transparent as Chrystal', and who, not long afterwards,
walked with him to the summit of a small hill, from whence
they were raised within a transparent column (or pillar) of fire
to heaven. The monk then awoke, and was so upset at being
back in the world that 'he started up like a mad man, and call'd
for his Bridge, and his meadow, without either speaking or
thinking of any thing else; and there was no perswading of
him to believe that he was any longer in his Cell'.
  The monk's experience might easily be dismissed as a vivid
dream were it not for the fact that two or three days later news
of Johann Reuchlin's death reached the convent, and it was
learned that he had left this vale of tears 'at the very instant of
this appearance to the Holy Man'. We must wonder if it was

143

purely coincidental that the monk went to sleep then, which allowed him to vacate his body in his double form and so meet the wraith of Reuchlin, or if his post-matins tiredness and the sleep that followed were somehow psychically generated by his dying friend.

It is to be regretted that Erasmus did not record what the river seen by the monk looked like. According to the Reverend Simpson, the river to which the sailor was conducted who collapsed when he tried to row back to the Isle of Man (see chapter 5), was not the same as the foul black one described by St Gregory's soldier, although it did flank a somewhat similar paradise:

The angel after this led me to a beautiful river, at the other side of which, in a flowery garden, I saw a great number of people, (chiefly Methodists) . . . and I saw a large gate, at the end of the field, which was studded over with diamonds, and out of the key-hole the rays of the sun shone so bright, that my eyes were quite dazzled.

The sailor did not, however, try to cross the river, for upon seeing the gate, his recovery (and return to consciousness) began when a white dove emerged from the bright key-hole, flew straight at him and struck him 'with force upon the breast'.

The sailor's experience is similar to that of a middle-aged modern American woman with a heart complaint, who told the doctor who resuscitated her that while unconscious she had seen 'a beautiful garden with a gate'. She also insisted that she had met God in the garden, accompanied by an angel, although no mention was made of what he had looked like.

The paradisial landscape which is often the departed wraith's first sighting of the next world was more fully described by Henry Webb, the reprobate whom we first met in the last chapter. As we saw, on Monday, 12 February 1750, he suffered a severe blood loss at his lodgings in Beaulieu, Hampshire, when a blood-letting incision made in his arm

earlier that day reopened. Those who found his blood-stained
body wanted to lay him immediately out for burial, but were
prevented from doing so by his employer, Mr Thomas Eades,
who detected a slight warmth in him, and who insisted that he
be left as he was until he became quite cold. Three days later,
the apparently lifeless man surprised everyone by groaning
and then opening his eyes. He had returned from the dead.
The following is a description by John Tregortha, based on
Henry's own recollection, of what he experienced when he
passed out:

He seemed to himself to be dying or fainting away, or rather his
soul going out of his body . . . He seemed to go into fields inex-
pressibly delightful and pleasant, beautiful with streams and foun-
tains of water clearer than crystal, having at the same time a glorious prospect of heaven before him, to which he directed his steps,
not once thinking upon this world, or reflecting on the heinousness
of his sins: after some time, he seemed to arrive at the gates of
heaven.

In 1801, a 22-year-old Welsh woman who lived with her
parents in Swansea was struck down by fever. This became so
serious that her doctors eventually gave up on her, telling her
parents that there was nothing further they could do and that
she would certainly die. The young woman subsequently
lapsed into a coma which mimicked death, and preparations
were made for her funeral.

But then, when all hope had gone, the woman returned to
life and was in due course restored to health and strength.
Some years later she wrote a poem describing her NDE,
which she had privately and anonymously printed. She did
not see any green fields when she left her body, but instead
had the following unique experience:

I found my spirit in a narrow lane,
I groaned, I wept, until my Saviour came
Riding on a colt; his robes were black,

145

His lovely chestnut hair flowed down his back –
His countenance shone brighter than the morn –
His eyes beamed pity on a wretch forlorn.

The very idea of the woman meeting Jesus riding on a horse
in the next world is so bizarre that it surely accurately reflects
what she saw, rather than being something she imagined. And
while she does not describe the landscape bordering the
'narrow lane', she did, upon being shown the distressing
sights of hell, find herself amid otherworldly fields when she
was sent back to her body.

Unto the earth my spirit did return,
Doom'd in this clay a few more years to mourn,
By pastures green, surpris'd, I did alight,
When soon a flood of water caught my sight,
On which, with great velocity, I moved
After my evil deeds had been reproved.
At length into those floods I seem'd to sink,
Where I was going I could no wise think;
The swelling waves rose high above my head,
And with a sigh, I op'd my eyes in bed.

Some people, of course, may find the idea of Jesus being clad
in a black robe offensive, while others might think that if the
woman did see such a figure, then it was a devil in disguise and
not the real Jesus. But the latter suggestion is discounted by
the fact that the black-robed Saviour gave the woman some
distinctly undevilish advice about how she should live when
she returned to her body, which suggests that his identity was
entirely bona fide:

'Follow,' he cried, 'the footsteps of your Lord,
And in your heart observe the living word.'

Other afterlife personages have also been encountered
wearing black, such as the monk-like figure mentioned by

146

John Aubrey in his *Miscellanies*, who came to a 'poor Widow's Daughter' of Hertfordshire, when she lapsed into a coma brought on by sickness in 1670. Kneeling beside the unconscious girl, her distraught mother begged God to take her instead, much as Alcestis had tried to take the place of Admetus. Then, when the daughter came to herself,

. . . She declared the vision she had in this Fit, vie, That one in black Habit came to her, whose face was so bright and glorious she could not behold it; and also he had such brightness upon his Breast, and (if I forget not) upon his Arms; and told her, That her Mother's Prayers were heard; and that her Mother should shortly die, and she should suddenly recover: And she did so, and her Mother died.

The appearance of a horse in the afterlife may sound implausible, but the anonymous Welsh woman is not the only person to have seen one. Indeed, Robert Bloynan – or simply Bloynan, as he prefers to call himself – had an even more remarkable equine encounter in May 1994, when he found himself riding a horse during a visit to a heavenly landscape. This happened during the two and a half days the 37-year-old businessman spent in a coma at St Thomas's Hospital, London, caused by the several epileptic fits he had one Saturday while waiting to have a brain tumour removed. Although Bloynan remembered nothing, including his own name, when he came round on the following Monday evening, by Wednesday he recalled having had a remarkable other-world experience.

I woke up in the next world riding a horse along the edge of a field of ripe corn. Two farmers were at the far end cutting the corn with scythes; there was a tree in the middle of the top side of the field which was bounded by a thick green hedge. The colours were astonishingly bright and vibrant. It was all solid but its material was more refined. There was no compulsion at all in this world. Everything and everyone was there and doing what they were doing because they chose to. The corn, the hedges and trees grew

147

because they wanted to. The horse was carrying me because it had chosen to, directly and without external pressure. All communication, including with the horse, was done by telepathy; there was no need to speak.

Part of Bloynan's 'enhanced cognitive functioning', as his heightened awareness is called, included a profound sense of having at last truly come home. Yet he was still aware of who he was.

My mind felt completely at home in that world. It was where I belonged. Everything was more 'real' and alive than in the material world. There was no difference in my sense of identity, only that my mind was operating in a much easier and more natural environment . . . It was like coming up for air after being under water for too long.

A striking other-world journey which closely resembles Bloynan's experience happened in 1965 to a 36-year-old woman named Mary Errington of Washington, Tyne and Wear, following an operation to repair a brain aneurysm. After losing consciousness when she was given an anaesthetic, the first thing Mrs Errington became aware of again was finding herself floating up near the ceiling of an unknown room, looking down at her physical self lying on a bed. She saw that her head was swathed in two large pressure bandages and that two nurses were anxiously bending over her. Then all of a sudden, she rose swiftly up through a large, dark-brown tunnel, towards the bright, white light at its end.

And then I went into this meadow. It was a vast meadow, with thick, luscious grass everywhere – apart from this one tree which I could see in the distance. And I could associate with it; I'd never really thought of trees before, but this one was friendly, that's the only thing I can say. I wasn't walking in the meadow; I was just floating gently towards this tree at the far side of the meadow. And the quietness . . . it can only be described as a heavenly silence

. . . The branches of the tree were like outstretched arms. It felt welcoming. And I felt that I had to go to the tree. I was nearly there. I could almost put out my hands to touch it. And then suddenly I was coming back down the tunnel very fast, and I was watching the doctors and nurses again, bringing me back to life.

Quite soon she recovered consciousness and found that the nurses were gently rubbing her eyes with ice, trying to reduce their swelling and the associated bruising. The next day, at her request, they brought her a mirror, which enabled her to see that the bandaging around her head was exactly the same as she had witnessed from the ceiling. The layout and the furniture of the recovery room, where she had never been before, were also the same. Taken together, they were evidence that her out-of-body experience had really happened. She is also quite sure that her visit to the meadow was not a dream, but a real event. 'When I die,' she adds, 'I think I'll go back to that meadow, and I think I'll reach the tree this time.'

The glorious meadow that Mrs Errington saw was similar to the cornfield in which Bloynan found himself riding a horse, except that it spread out uniformly in every direction and had no hedges. There was no road either that she had to walk along, but instead she found herself floating over the grass towards a distant tree. Nor was there any sign of a garden, although the trees in both cases, and Bloynan's hedges, formed suitable substitutes, especially as Mrs Errington's tree seemed to be aware of her approach and had a friendly, welcoming personality. This tree probably represented the end point to life, so had she reached it and touched its branches, she might not have been able to return to her body, much like those who cross the more familiar river or wall.

When 34-year-old Matthew Robinson of Market Harborough in Leicestershire returned home late from a visit to Mount Sorrel, near Leicester, on Sunday, 3 November 1821, he had no inkling of the desperate state he was in. Indeed, he felt 'remarkably lively', which he put down to the joyous effect of the church service he had attended. But after eating something he began to feel very faint and weak, much to the consternation of his poor wife, who had to call in a neighbour to help her get him into bed. Not long afterwards Matthew lapsed into a deep trance, from which he did not wake for three days, although when he finally came to his senses he had a remarkable story to tell. In fact it was evident that he had left his body and been taken to the next world. In his account, *The Wonderful Trance of Matthew Robinson*, he writes:

About three o'clock on the following morning I fell into a Trance, and was immediately transported to a wide and fertile plain, where I saw no person near me. After looking around some time, I observed an elderly and venerable person at a little distance, clad in a loose and flowing garment. He approached me with a cheerful smile, and waved a light silver wand for me to follow him. I instantly did so, and he conducted me by a narrow path into a delightful grove, where every air was balm, and every sound the most enchanting melody. 'This Son,' said my guide, 'is the place where the souls of the living saints meet in converse with God.'

The numerous views of heavenly gardens are significant, but what are we to make of the NDE of an elderly college-educated, female heart-attack victim, which Drs Osis and Erlender include in their book *At the Hour of Death*? The woman's doctor said:

She told me that a taxi driver had taken her to a beautiful garden where she saw beautiful, endless gardens, all kinds of flowers. She said she had never seen anything like it, it was gorgeous. She did not want to return, but the taxi driver was impatient to get started . . . She would go back there any day . . . It sounded like a dream to me, but it seemed real to her.

The woman's unusual form of transport was also a feature of the vivid and apparently entirely real time travel visit, which I described in *Doubles: The Enigma of the Second Self*, that *The*

Times journalist Peter Ackroyd had in 1996. While asleep one night he suddenly found himself inside a house in Kensington in the year 1858. His visit there, however, ended in a rather startling way. 'I left the house and there, to my astonishment (and, I must say, slight unease) was a street of the mid-19th century, with the doors, façades and areas exactly as they once had been. My dream ended rather abruptly when a late 20th century London taxi pulled up.'

An early case involving the sighting of a paradisial tree similar to that seen by Mrs Errington is related by Roger of Wendover. He describes how, on Friday, 27 October 1206, an Essex peasant farmer named Turchill fell into a profound sleep or trance lasting for two days, during which his double or soul was led away to the 'middle of the world' by St Julian. There they entered a vast church, whose roof was supported by only three pillars and which was 'without partitions', so that in size and open plan it resembled the magnificent church of St Sophia, the Church of Holy Wisdom, at Constantinople (modern Istanbul). Brightly lit by a large, centrally placed non-burning flame, the church served as the assembly point for all newly separated wraiths, whence they were sent either to hell or to heaven. The wraiths of the just and good, Turchill noticed, were white in colour and had youthful faces, whereas those which had led sinful lives displayed black and white spots, the more evil being blacker than the rest, and their faces were ugly and deformed.

St Julian then gave Turchill a lengthy tour of hell, whose entrance lay to one side of the church, wherein he saw the punishments meted out to different types of sinner. Afterwards he was taken to an exterior 'mount of joy', where there was a temple to which the white wraiths were conducted by St Michael, where they would live. A lovely garden formed part of the temple precinct.

They turned aside to the eastern part of the aforesaid temple, and came to a most pleasant place, beautiful in the variety of its herbs and flowers, and filled with the sweet smell of herbs and trees; there the man beheld a very clear spring, which sent forth four streams of different coloured water; over this fountain there was a beautiful tree of wondrous size and immense height, which abounded in all kinds of fruits and in the sweet smell of spices. Under this tree near the fountain there reposed a man of comely form and gigantic body . . . 'This,' said St Michael, 'is the first parent of the human race, Adam.'

We noted in chapter 4 that Adam, according to the *Questions of Bartholomew*, was released from Hades by Jesus, who vanished from the cross during the three-hour period of eclipse in order to 'harrow hell'. Hades himself was overthrown and chained up, although his place was taken by the fallen angel Beliar, who quickly became known by his newly acquired name of Satan. The freed Adam was carried up to heaven by angels, and if Turchill is to be believed, he has since resided in the wonderful paradisial landscape described.

In ancient times trees were worshipped throughout Europe, where they were the principal feature of the landscape, greatly outnumbering people and providing them with the bulk of their food, fuel and building materials. Impressively large in size, their roots reached far down into the soil/underworld, while their uplifted branches caressed the heavens. Not only were they seemingly in communion with the gods, but each tree was thought to be the home of a spirit or dryad, which made them doubly holy and worthy of worship. Only fools or those who were tired of life damaged or cut down trees, for divine retribution would be sure to follow such an impious act.

The verbal abuse of trees was also dangerous, as indeed it sometimes is still. This was demonstrated as recently as 1972, when a 72-year-old retired secretary named Elizabeth Stevens, of Norcross, Gwinnet County, Georgia, was killed by the fall of a 100-foot pine tree. Mrs Stevens hated the tree, which stood about 15 feet from her bedroom, not least because it shed needles and pine cones on her neatly manicured back lawn and swayed threateningly when the winds were high. She regularly reviled it to her neighbours and often spoke about having it cut down, although the expense prevented her from doing so. However, it was Mrs Stevens's oft-repeated wish to die peacefully in bed that seemingly prompted the tree's gruesome revenge, for when it was toppled during a bad storm in early April of that year, it fell on her bedroom and crushed her to death while she slept.

The Teutons believed that all spiritual and physical life was sustained by a great tree known as Yggdrasill or the World Tree, which grew at the world's centre and whose branches spread out protectively over all. Said to be an ash tree, Yggdrasill was nevertheless always in leaf, and each time a leaf fell from it the person died whose name was written on the leaf. And likewise, when a new leaf grew on the tree, a child was born. Thus Yggdrasill, in this respect, was the tree of fate, rather like the tree that Mary Errington had floated towards, for had she reached it she knew she could not have returned to her body and to life. And of course it is doubly ironic that Elizabeth Stevens was killed by a tree when trees in general are such a positive force for good.

We have thus far noted that the NDE of being in a field or a garden is not only frequently reported, but is of ancient vintage. This raises the question of whether or not the experience occurs as a post-mortem recapitulation of an old, yet powerful and recurring idea – that of a safe, beautiful haven surrounded by that which is barren and inhospitable? The contrast was stark in the early Middle East, where gardening as we know it began, for the walled gardens of Mesopotamia were enclaves of cool, green, flowery delight encircled by the hot, dry, dusty desert. And even today, many people find a similar contrast between the ordered beauty of their garden and the world outside, with its noise, dirt, rush and disorder, which together comprise chaos. Or as Abraham Cowley (1618–67) put it:

> Oh blessed shades! O gentle cool retreat
> From all th' immoderate heat,

153

In which the frantic world doth burn and sweat!

We can therefore postulate that when the brain, through illness or accident, is starved of oxygen and dying, and consciousness finds itself threatened on all sides by an encroaching darkness and nothingness, it might spontaneously generate comforting scenes of beauty, freshness and life in the form of imagined fields and gardens. It has the creative power to do this, and the possibility is supported by the fact that the percentage of those who report having seen a field or a garden roughly matches the proportion of gardeners in the population, although no one to my knowledge has asked those who apparently found themselves in a garden if they are members of the green thumb brigade.

And if NDE returnees protest that the quality and the intensity of their experience clearly distinguishes it from a dream, we might argue that their impressions were heightened by the fact that the conditions within their brains were *in extremis*, so to speak, in the same way that the greatest pain produces the loudest, shrillest scream.

It was this doubt that prompted Henry Watts' sister to ask him if he could give her 'any certain Testimony for human Satisfaction, of his being in another World'. As we have seen he did so by relating 'some Secret sins' that she had committed, which were apparently revealed to him along with his own. Others have had similar doubts, although these were usually, and if true convincingly, dispelled by the recovered person recalling having seen on the other side the wraiths of those who actually died while he or she was unconscious. The soldier mentioned by St Gregory is one case in point. When brought to the brink of death, he had suddenly found himself by a bridge over a black, foul-smelling river, where he saw the wraith of Stephen, who unbeknowst to himself had died earlier that same day. Similarly, the German monk saw his friend Johann Reuchlin cross another otherworldly bridge, but it was only much later that news came of Reuchlin's simultaneous death.

Another interesting early example was reported in the
Ladies' Dictionary (1694) and involved a 14-year-old girl
named Anna Atherton, who after suffering a long illness fell
into a death-like trance which lasted seven days, during which
she claimed she was taken to the gates of heaven (about which
more is related in the next chapter), and who, to quieten those
who doubted she had seen such things,

. . . told them of three or four Persons that were dead since she was
deprived of her senses, and named each Person; (one of them was
dead, and they knew not of it before they sent to enquire:) She
said, *She saw them passing by her, while she stood at the Gate.*
One of those She named was reputed a vicious Person, came as
afar as the Gate, but was sent back again another way. All the
Persons she named, died in the time she lay in this Trance.

But if such scenic landscapes are real in the sense that the
observer is located within them in his double or wraith form
just as he might physically stand in an earthly garden or field,
why do they show so much variety? We have noted, for
instance, that the Mesopotamian garden of the setting sun
contained 'bushes bearing gems'; that the Greek Elysium
consisted of broad green meadows, orchards and gardens; that
the garden of the Hesperides was a walled orchard located on
a mountain; that Er found himself in a sunlit meadow stretch-
ing as far as the eye could see; that some landscapes include
beautiful shining buildings while others have none; that some
have streams and rivers but others do not; that one river was
foul and smelly, whereas most are fresh and pure; that some
gardens are distinguished by the sweetness of their odours,
others by the abundance of their fruits; that one lush meadow
contained a wonderful tree; and that some heavenly fields are
empty of people, some contain a few people, and some very
many people.

One possible answer to this conundrum is given by
Emanuel Swedenborg (1688–1772) in his book *Heaven and
Hell.* Swedenborg, a gifted mathematician, engineer and scien-

tist, was also blessed with outstanding psychic and visionary abilities, and he even resigned from his post at Stockholm's College of Mines in 1747 to promote his spiritual revelations. He claimed to have had many direct viewings of the next world, including meetings and conversations with angels. The fact that his description of the initial stages of life after death is similar to that related by many who have had an NDE suggests that his opinions are worth considering.

Swedenborg said that the wraiths or spirits of the newly dead retain their physical appearance and mannerisms, and that they are first taken to 'an intermediate place between heaven and hell', where they are examined and judged before being sent either up to heaven or down to hell. Their stay in the intermediate place may be very brief or it may last for as long as thirty years. Where they go next, as we might expect, depends upon how they lived their lives on earth.

The nature of the intermediate place in which they find themselves corresponds to their ruling love or delight in life. Those who have 'lived in the world of heavenly love' therefore choose landscapes that are light and open. Two of these light-filled vistas contain almost all of the countryside features mentioned above. Moreover, because they are apparently vast in extent, what is seen in them will vary according to which part of the landscape the wraith is taken to and the length of time that he or she stays there. To those who have loved divine truths and the Word from interior affection in life,

. . . there are presented to their view as it were fields and standing corn, and also vineyards. Everything in their houses glitters as if made of precious stones; when they look through the windows, it is as through pure crystals . . . for the truths from the Word, which they have loved, correspond to standing corn, vineyards, precious stones, windows, and crystals.

Alternatively, if they have been attracted, like Swedenborg, to science and have used their love of discovery to acquire intelligence and gain understanding while at the same time

acknowledging the divine, then their corresponding intermediate landscape is somewhat different:

They dwell in gardens, in which are seen beds of flowers and
garden-plots beautifully arranged, surrounded by rows of trees
with arbours and walks. The trees and flowers vary every day . . .
These are their delights, because gardens, beds of flowers, lawns,
and trees, correspond to sciences, to knowledge, and intelligence
therefrom.

But for those who have lived less than worthy lives the intermediate landscapes are correspondingly darker and more
forbidding.

All those who are in evil, and have confirmed themselves in falsi-
ties against the truths of the Church, especially those who have
rejected the Word, shun the light of heaven, and rush into hiding-
places, which at their openings appear very dark, and into clefts
of rocks where they hide themselves . . . It is their delight to dwell
there, and undelightful to them to dwell in open fields.

For those who have behaved in different reprehensible ways,
the landscapes vary according to their sins. Thus all who have
schemed and plotted against other people find themselves in
'rooms so dark that they cannot even see one another'; those
who have studied science merely to appear learned and have
'taken delight in the things of memory from pride therein' end
up in a barren, sandy landscape; those who have learned
Church doctrine but without applying it to their lives 'choose
rocky places, and dwell among heaps of stones'; those who
were hedonists and gluttons find themselves in dunghills and
privies; those who were besotted with wealth and material
possessions 'dwell in cells, and love the filth of swine'; while
the adulterous and lascivious, adds Swedenborg, 'dwell in the
other world in brothels, where all things are vile and filthy'.
These iniquities are of course essentially the traditional
seven deadly sins, and we can pick out pride, gluttony, envy,

avarice and lust without difficulty, although hypocrisy seems to have taken the place of anger and sloth. Yet although these worldly traits are wrong, it is difficult to understand why Swedenborg makes no direct mention of such far more serious crimes as rape, robbery and murder.

The dark, rocky landscape to which Swedenborg saw religious hypocrites consigned raises questions about the life of Carl Jung. It will be remembered that following a heart attack, Jung suddenly found himself out in space looking down at the earth. He then 'noticed a huge block of dark stone floating near him', which he entered. And within the rock Jung had an important insight into himself. He learned that although he liked to pose as a wise old buffer interested only in elucidating the nature of the human mind, work which had required him to examine many myths and religious beliefs, he was as hypocritically driven by ambition and status as the next man.

And what about the landscape visited by a 72-year-old Oxford professor, an eminent literary scholar, during the NDE he had at the Royal Marsden Hospital, London, in March 1983? The elderly academic, who was undergoing treatment for a lymphoma in his neck, had been given a routine diagnostic lumbar puncture but 20 minutes later was found to be comatose and unrousable. Yet because the procedure had required neither a sedative nor an anaesthetic, his attendant visionary experience was not drug-induced. His description of the barren scene in which he found himself forms part of the account by him included in a paper by Ian Judson and E. Wiltshaw, published in *The Lancet*:

Scene: high plateau; rocks; the ground is level, sandy; no trees or other vegetation; a tall rock, resembling a dolmen, stands off-centre. Colour of the ground, rock; sky: a uniform pale gold. Background: not dark, but vague.

I am standing 'in the shadow' (but there are no shadows here) of the great rock. My shape is more or less that of a cube, but is in the process of transformation, perhaps towards a globe. I am a living being, and my life is bliss and utter rightness, but a greater bliss and discovery of being are imminent. I rest in and open myself to the power which is within and about me.

Hence the professor not only visited a barren landscape both sandy and rocky, but he was also seemingly a part of it, having acquired, as he says, a cubical shape, rather like a lump of carved rock. This would have made him, according to Swedenborg, redolent with pride and hypocrisy, which may of course have been true, as the groves of academe are notorious for stimulating base desires. But if so, why did he feel in a state of 'bliss and utter rightness' with evidently even more of the same to follow? And why was there no darkness or shadows?

That no 'greater bliss and discovery of being' ensued was due to the fact that his resuscitation was begun with a 0.4 mg intravenous injection of naloxone. This turned his wonderful experience into a painful and protracted fight with the medical team, who were, as he saw it, trying to drag him forcibly from the place where he wanted to be. Indeed, the doctors noted that 'within a minute he awoke, looking extremely frightened, and began to struggle violently'. The professor ended his account of the event by saying:

I am still in terror of the doctors and the evil nurse their accomplice. I still have hopes of escape for a return to my own world. I see the hospital as the focus of some monstrous conspiracy, their patients as deluded victims. I am back in my science fiction world, the world of kidnappings, of enslavement to some unknown but cruel purpose. I wake up each morning to this fear, this bewilderment . . . It speaks for the appalling intensity of the original experience that only after two or three days of routine hospital existence did I come fully to accept the sane version of what had happened.

He subsequently felt ashamed at having so negatively viewed the activities of the medical team, but when he learned later that he only had two or three months left to live, he was determined to avoid the same thing happening again. 'When I go this time,' he said, 'I don't want them pulling me back.' He therefore resolved to end his treatment and go to his villa in Crete to die.

7

At Heaven's Gate

This was done; and in about half an hour, the young man gave signs of returning life: till at last he was able to utter, 'I am in heaven'. But his blood was so thoroughly chilled by the exposure of his body . . . that every restorative measure, which could be used, proved ineffectual.

Last moments of Charles Holland, actor,
who died of smallpox in 1769

Heaven is the place where the wraiths or souls of the just and the good dwell after death. It apparently lies, as we have seen, somewhere 'outside this world' and it consists of two principal regions, to wit, a vast, varied and beautiful landscape or paradise, which surrounds an even more wonderful area enclosed, as some have reported, by a high golden wall. Passage through the wall is via a magnificent gate. Wraiths reach the heavenly gate by hiking along the 'smooth road' leading to it. Entry to the gate, however, is usually restricted to those whose physical bodies are irreversibly dead, which is why most NDE visitants see only what is visible from it. Such exclusion from heaven's interior implies that the accounts given of the wall and the gate are true, for if the NDE is only a dream, then why have so few dreamed of going through the gate?

The writer of the *Apocalypse of Paul* claimed that within the golden wall stood eleven other walls, concentrically arranged, which together encircled, but also formed part of, the city of Christ. Most returnees, however, do not report seeing any inner walls. And while some say that there is a mansion or palace and other buildings standing just within the gate, others have seen no interior structures at all. This discrepancy may either mean that the wall has more than one gate or that what is seen from it varies.

The brash placement of heaven 'outside this world', if by that we mean within our surrounding airy envelope, is almost certainly wrong. 'Out in space' is a more likely location, especially as such airless heights were visited by the wraiths of Carl Jung and St Fursey, both of whom were able to look down on the world far below them, although neither claimed to be in heaven. Of more relevance is the otherworldly experience of the monk St Salvius, mentioned in chapter 5, whose separated wraith was 'carried away and taken to heaven by angels', where he had had 'beneath my feet not only this muddy earth, but also the sun and moon, the clouds and the stars', which makes it plain that he was well outside the Earth's atmosphere. He was then led into a huge and marvellous building 'filled by an ineffable light, wherein there was a floor resplendent with gold and silver' on which was gathered a vast crowd of wraiths.

But while the house (or mansion) into which Salvius was taken resembles that mentioned in later accounts of heaven, none of them portrays it as floating freely in space. Most wraiths in fact find themselves walking through the paradisial landscape to heaven's gate. This probably means that paradise, the golden wall and its gate are quasi-physical phantoms like our double form, which are not seen and experienced by everyone. So perhaps those who are highly developed spiritually or especially close to God, like St Salvius, do not need the reassurance of such sights to help them cope with the first stages of death.

Not long after Salvius arrived in the glorious house, he learned to his dismay that he was to be sent back to his body:

When the angels that preceded me had made a path through the throng, we arrived at a place that we had already seen from afar

162

and above which was suspended a cloud brighter than all light; we could not distinguish either the sun or the moon, or any star, and it shone by its own brightness more than all the stars; from the cloud came a voice resembling the sound of mighty waters . . . Standing at the place they indicated, I was suffused with a perfume of exquisite sweetness, which nourished me in such a way that I felt no more hunger or thirst. I heard the voice say: 'He may return to earth, for he is necessary to the churches.' I heard only the voice, because we could not see him who spoke . . . Having then left my companions, I descended in tears, and left where I had entered.

Such aerial uplifts to heaven are rare, although the wraith of the Reverend Jeremiah Carter apparently went one giant step further. For when he collapsed on that remote north Lancashire bridle-path, he was carried aloft by 'the Angel of the Lord . . . under the Shadow of his Wings' and taken to the heaven of heavens, where he saw 'the Ancient of Days sitting on his glorious Throne, and the Lord Jesus sitting at his Right Hand'. But while neither divine personage is described, much less their surroundings, the vicar did add: 'No Tongue can express the Happiness of the Saints above. There I beheld Thousands of glorious Angels, and Souls departed, in white Robes, wearing everlasting Crowns of Glory. I saw so much Splendour, and heard such heavenly Songs of divers Praises and Hallelujahs to the Saviour of the World.' However, it is very unusual – and scarcely believable – for anyone to be taken to the 'heaven of heavens', which is none other than 'Paul's' seventh heaven where God himself supposedly resides. The wraiths of the departed can in reality only expect to reach what our anonymous author called the third heaven.

Another experience of being carried aloft to a similar featureless, angel-filled heaven happened to Richard Langly, a widowed glazier of Ratcliffe Highway (now The Highway) in East London, when he fell into a death-like trance or coma, caused by consumption, on Wednesday 5 February 1708. The coma lasted for thirty-six hours, and was only ended when Richard was moved and manipulated by those laying him out.

His aerial adventure was described in a chap-book printed shortly afterwards, which noted:

Being (as he thought) fetch'd by two Angels away from the Earth, they carry'd him with an unexpressible swiftness to Heaven's Gates, the Glory whereof, when he was enter'd, far exceeded the Description given of it by St John in his Revelations. The Inhabitants of this Glorious Mansion were Seraphims, and Cherubims, Archangels, and Angels, accompanied with Holy Spirits, Blessed Apostles, and Victorious Martyrs; who with Palms in their Hands, and Crowns on their Heads, were singing Hallelujahs to the King of Kings, Blessed for evermore.

Richard Langly was fortunate to be taken through the gates of heaven, as most visitants are kept outside them. The 'Glorious Mansion' or dwelling place that he entered, however, clearly resembles that visited by St Salvius, which may mean that they are the same.

A somewhat fuller description of what she saw outside heaven's wall is given by Mary Stone, who died from the ague in September 1757, but who was restored to life in her coffin three days later by her mother's farewell kiss. Mary had no memory of being carried up into the sky, but said she suddenly found herself in the next world, where a white-robed guide obligingly gave her an introductory tour. After first showing her hell and its screaming inhabitants, he then led her into a far more pleasant region:

From thence we went to the right hand a day or two more, where I came to a place, the most glorious to my sight that was ever of eyes beheld; the walls to my sight were pure glittering beaten gold, and I heard the most ravishing melodious music, which no tongue can express the sweetness of. This place, says my guide, is the celestial Jerusalem, where dwells the Holy of Holies, a place prepared of ever-lasting rest and happiness for those that live a godly life . . . I asked of my guide and comforter if I should enter in that most glorious place: and he said, No, not then, for I must go from whence I came.

But while Mary seems to have been taken to the golden-walled city of Christ, she makes no mention of an outer river or lake, nor of any towers, gates or inner walls. But she did hear some 'ravishing melodious music', much as 'Paul' ostensibly heard the singing of 3,000 angels when he was rowed across Lake Acherusa. This similarity may mean either that Mary unconsciously recalled as a visual hallucination what little she knew about the celestial city of the *Apocalypse of Paul* or that she actually saw what she said she did. If the latter, it also suggests the *Apocalypse* was based on some unknown person's near-death experience.

We noted in chapter 6 that Henry Webb also visited a heavenly gate, although he saw nothing scenic within it.

After some time, he seemed to arrive at the gates of heaven, which shone more glorious and bright than the sun in its greatest lustre: he knocked at the gates, which were immediately opened to him, and he saw within, three men in bright and shining clothing, far exceeding every thing he had ever seen, and more glorious than he can express; two of them came out to him, and the gates were immediately shut again: he entreated these two men in shining clothes admittance in at the gate, but was told by them, 'it was not a place for any such wicked sinners as he was.'

More revealing is the experience of Turchill, the Essex peasant farmer whom we also met in the last chapter, whose double left his body when he fell into a profound sleep and was taken to a church at the 'middle of the world' by St Julian. After the saint had shown Turchill the horrors of hell, they were joined by St Michael, who conducted them to a temple on the flank of the nearby 'mount of joy'. Beside the temple was a beautiful garden wherein reclined Adam, the first man.

After proceeding a little way from this place they came to a most beautiful gate adorned with jewels and precious stones; and the wall round it shone as if it were gold. As soon as they had entered the gate, there appeared a kind of golden temple, much more

magnificent than the former in all its beauty, in its pleasant sweetness, and in the splendour of its glittering light, so that the places
which they had seen before appeared not at all pleasant in
comparison with that place.

This description indicates that the gate was different from the
one seen by Henry Webb, which if true would mean that the
golden wall has more than one gate, although the 'kind of
golden temple' standing just inside it resembles the 'Glorious
Mansion' entered by Richard Langly and by St Salvius.

Beside the golden temple was a 'kind of chapel' in which
were seated three virgins 'shining in indescribable beauty'. St
Michael identified them as being St Catherine, St Margaret
and St Osith, all of whom had supposedly been martyred.
Then, as Turchill was admiring their stunning beauty, the
archangel suddenly instructed St Julian to return him quickly
to his body before it was choked by those trying to rouse him,
who were then throwing water in his face. 'And the man, not
knowing how, was brought back to his body and sat up in
bed.'

But while the 'most beautiful gate adorned with jewels and
precious stones' seen by Turchill appears to have been
heaven's gate, the church he first entered and the nearby
'mount of joy' were oddly located somewhere in the 'middle
of the world'. But in 1226, when his experience occurred, the
'middle of the world' was considered to be the city of
Constantinople, the capital of the Eastern Roman Empire,
where stood the magnificent church of St Sophia, built by
Emperor Justinian and consecrated in AD 537. The similarity
in the description suggests that Roger of Wendover may have
been inspired by reports of the church to include it in his
account of Turchill's heavenly visit. Also, while Saints
Catherine (of Alexandria), Margaret and Osith – and indeed
Julian – were very popular religious figures in the Middle
Ages, there is no evidence for them ever having existed, which
means that they would not really be found in heaven.

Moreover, if heaven's interior has a surrounding wall of

gold, then everyone who is brought to heaven's gate should see a golden wall. But surprisingly, this is not always the case. The monk of Evesham, for example, whose journey to heaven is also described by Roger of Wendover, saw the following vista when his guide, like Turchill's and Mary Stone's, conducted him first through hell and then through two places of rest and blessedness:

After proceeding for some distance, and as the pleasantness of the places before us increased, I saw what appeared a wall of crystal, which was so high that no one could look over it, and to the extent of which there was no end, and on our approaching it, I saw it glittered with a most shining brightness from within. I also saw the entrance to it open, but marked with the protecting sign of the cross; thither approached crowds of those who being near were very anxious to enter, and the cross in the middle of the gate now raising itself on high, opened an entrance to those who approached; afterwards, falling again, it denied admittance to those who wished to enter.

Having spent some time outside the gate, although for what reason is not made clear, the guide then passed inside. The Evesham monk attempted to follow him, but the cross came down to bar his way. Turning, the guide told him not to be afraid and to put his trust in God, which the monk did and so entered without further ado. But despite having passed through heaven's gate, we then learn that he could not see anything within owing to the brightness of the light – 'How glittering was the inconceivable brightness, or how strong was the light which filled all those places,' he said, 'let no one ask of me, for this I am not able to express in words, nor even to recollect in my mind.' – although he could discern the wall of crystal behind him and some 'steps of a wonderful beauty' leading up to its top, which those coming through the gate immediately climbed. They did this without effort, for 'the step above was always ascended more easily than the one below'. The monk continued:

And when I directed my eyes above, I beheld, sitting on a throne of glory, our Lord and Saviour in human form, and, as it seemed to me, the spirits of five or seven hundred blessed beings, who had lately ascended by the before-mentioned road to the place of the throne, coming round him in a circle, and with signs of thanksgiving worshipping him. But it was most evident to me, that the place which I saw was not the heaven of heavens, where the Lord of Lords will appear in Sion, as if he were in his majesty.

From this it is evident that the Evesham monk was also taken to heaven's interior, although how can we explain the wall of crystal seen by him, when so many others have come upon a golden one? The answer may lie with *The Revelation of St John the Divine*, the last New Testament book, written by the apostle John at Patmos in about AD 86. He describes therein the stunning vision he had of the end of the world and the Second Coming, which includes the descent of the city of Christ or the new Jerusalem from the third heaven. The city, according to John, 'shone like a precious stone, like a jasper, clear as crystal'. It was square in shape and its wall had a circumference of 12,000 furlongs or 1,500 miles and a height 216 of feet. The wall also had *twelve* gates, three in each of its four walls, and each made of a single pearl, hence the so-called 'pearly gates'. John further adds:

And the building of the wall *of* it was jasper: and the city *was* pure gold, like unto clear glass . . . the street of the city was pure gold, as it were transparent glass. And I saw no temple therein: for the Lord God Almighty and the Lamb are the temple of it. And the city had no need of the sun, neither of the moon, to shine in it: for the glory of God did lighten it, and the Lamb *is* the light thereof. (John, *Revelation*, XXI, 18, 21–3)

This obviously accords, in some degree at least, with what the monk of Evesham saw during his NDE. There is the jasper wall 'clear as crystal' and the divinely lit interior. And within this wall was a city, whose buildings and street, while made of gold, were transparent like glass, which would render them, one would think, very difficult to see. Their transparency also makes it hard to understand how St John could tell that they were made of gold. But if paradise and the wall of the inner heaven are quasi-physical phantoms, their appearance to the onlooker, as I have indicated above, may depend upon his or her spiritual development. Hence heavenly gold, if we may call it that, does not have the unvarying opacity of earthly gold, but can sometimes seem as transparent as crystal or glass.

The monk of Evesham, however, saw nothing within the light of heaven's interior, with the exception of the steps leading up the crystal wall, which are not mentioned by St John, and he only saw one gate, whose protective cross has no equivalent in John's city, and is not mentioned by our other visitants. This may mean that they went to other gates, or alternatively, if there is only one gate, that its form varies in accordance with the inner state of the wraith viewing it. And while it is odd that the monk, owing to the brightness of the interior light, saw nothing within except the wall and some steps, his claim that he found himself in a luminosity that 'inconceivable as it was, did not blind the eye-sight' is reminiscent of the light that many in modern times have reported entering into from the ubiquitous tunnel.

The experience of Anna Atherton, which was confirmed by her brother, a doctor of Caermarthen, is of particular interest. She fell sick with a feverish malaria-like illness in November 1669 and despite having the care of several physicians became steadily thinner, paler and weaker during the following weeks, until she apparently gave up the ghost in February 1670. However, the women who came to lay her out became doubtful about the reality of her death when they detected a slight warmth in her body, which persisted after they had cooled her bedroom by opening its windows. But when they held a mirror to Anna's mouth it did not mist over, which seemed to indicate that she was not breathing, and when they placed live coals on the soles of her feet they 'discovered not the least sign of Life or Sense'. Such unresponsiveness suggested of course that she really was dead.

But Anna's mother sensibly refused to have her daughter buried until all trace of body heat had disappeared, and she kept her at home in bed for the following seven days. In the seventeenth century this was an astonishingly long time to defer burial, particularly as virtually all trace of heat had vanished from her body by the seventh day. But then, to everyone's amazement, Anna's temperature suddenly increased, which prompted her carers to use friction and other resuscitative measures. These in due course gave rise to a faint but detectable pulse, then breathing, and at last a return to consciousness. And what was even more incredible, the girl came back from the dead in a state of excitement, requesting that her mother be brought to her bedside, to whom she then exclaimed:

Oh Mother! since I was absent from you, I have been in Heaven, an Angel went before me to conduct me thither: I passed through several Gates, and at length I came to Heaven's Gate, where I saw things very Glorious and Unutterable, as Saints, Angels, and the like, in glorious Apparel, and I heard unparalleled Musick, Divine Anthems and Hallelujahs.

I would fain have entered that glorious Place, but the Angel that went before me withstood me, yet I thought myself half in; but he told me, I could not be admitted now, but must go back and take leave of my Friends, and after some short time I should be admitted.

So he brought me hither again, and is standing at the Bed's-feet; Mother! you must needs see him, he is all in white. *Her Mother told her, it was but a Dream or Fancy, and that she knew not what she said. Whereupon she answered with a great deal of vehemency,* That it was as true as that she was there at present.

This transcription evokes the wonder felt by Anna and her obvious belief in the reality of her experience. Her words are those of a girl hurriedly recounting what had happened to her, which bespeaks their veracity. Anna surely gave a more detailed and considered description of what she saw and heard later on, and probably repeated it many times, but it seems that on those occasions there was no literate person at her bedside to take down what she said. Two years later, as her guide had indicated, she died 'in great Assurance of her salvation, speaking comfortable words, and giving wholesome instruction to all who came to visit her'.

Although Anna was met by a guide, whom she calls an angel, it is unclear whether that meeting happened here or in the next realm. And unlike the monk of Evesham, Mary Stone and others, she was not taken on the usual tour of hell but instead straight to heaven. There she passed through several gates before reaching 'Heaven's Gate', which suggests that she was led through those of the concentrically arranged walls of the 'Pauline' city of Christ. But she was not permitted to enter the last gate, for she had to return to her body, although the fact that she got that far says much about her innate goodness (despite having 'a brisk and Lively Temper') and her belief in God, to whom she prayed throughout her illness. Indeed, the fact she was not shown hell suggests that her loving nature was discernible to her guide, who knew it would render her safe from the temptations of the world on her return.

That Anna's guide accompanied her wraith back to her body and remained in the room while she recovered consciousness is unusual. Moreover, because she could see the white-robed figure at the end of her bed, despite it being invisible to her mother, further indicates that what she experienced in heaven was not a dream, for dream figures do not persist into everyday reality when someone awakes.

As I mentioned in the last chapter, Anna also saw several people at the heavenly gate who had died while she lay in her coma. The previewing of people's wraiths in this way before it is known they have died is quite often reported. Less frequently the visitant may be told of those in his (or her) household or locality who are soon to die, and this prophecy, when repeated on his return to his body, becomes a verification of his otherworldly experience when their deaths show it to be true.

John Beaumont gives an example of this in his treatise on spirits and apparitions (1705), although it is taken from a Latin work written by Johannes Marcus Marci which has proved impossible to track down. The boy, who was evidently an apprentice in Rome, was thought to have died of the plague, but then surprised everyone by suddenly coming back to life. 'Calling his Master, [he] told him he had really been in Heaven, and there had understood how many, and who were to die out the House, and naming them; he affirm'd his Master should survive, and to create a belief in what he said, he shew'd that he had learn'd all languages.' The boy in fact was able to speak fluent Greek with his master, despite having no previous knowledge of the language, and to converse with others in a variety of foreign languages, which was sufficiently wonderful to amaze them all. He survived no more than three days, however, his death happening in consequence of him 'falling into a Rage' wherein he apparently 'lay'd hold of his Hands with his Teeth, and really died; and the others whom he had nam'd died, his Master remaining alive'.

The next case of a person visiting heaven dates from the early eighteenth century and is truly extraordinary. Its singularity derives from the fact that its subject, Nicholas (or Klaas) Hart, not only regularly fell into a deep trance on the same date every year, but always left his body and made his way to heaven's gate. Such regularly repeated trances are not without precedent. St Catherine of Palma (d. 1574), for example, became entranced every year for two weeks immediately prior to the feast of the afore-mentioned St Catherine of Alexandria, which falls on 25 November, when she recovered her senses. St Catherine of Palma not only left her body during her trance and visited Palestine and other earthly places, but she was also taken aloft to heaven.

The reason for Nicholas Hart's annual descent into insensibility may lie with the circumstances of his birth, for his mother fell into a trance some twenty-four hours prior to his birth at Leyden, in Holland, on 5 August 1689, and remained in that state for the following three days. Thereafter, on each birthday, Nicholas routinely lapsed into unconsciousness, the trance lasting one day longer than his mother's and was impossible to break. However, when he did wake up, and having satisfied his thirst by drinking two or three pints of cold water, he insisted on telling those gathered around him what had happened to his disembodied double while he lay entranced, which always went to heaven's gate, although the wraiths he saw there were different on each visit, as we would expect if his experience was genuine. But strangely, the length of time that Nicholas thought he was at heaven's gate never seemed longer than about two hours to him 'because of the ravishing delights of the place'. This time discrepancy has also been reported by those who have visited the fairy realm.

Nicholas's childhood was made unhappy by the jealousy of his two brothers, who did all that they could to turn his father, the mathematician and astronomer John (or Jan) Hart – and a former tutor of William, Prince of Orange – against him. Family tensions eventually became so bad that in the summer of 1701, at age twelve, Nicholas one night ran away from home, made his way to Amsterdam, and joined the crew of the *Nassau*, which was about to depart on a three-and-a-half-year voyage to the East Indies. When he returned to Holland, he continued to follow the seaman's life, although 'every 5th day of August, in every year, be he aboard or on shore', he always fell into a trance lasting five days and nights. This meant of course that he had to warn his captain and shipmates of what was going to happen to him, although once this peculiarity was known about, it was generally accepted and tolerated.

But problems occurred for him in 1708, when the Dutch vessel he was then aboard was first captured by a French ship and then retaken shortly afterwards by an English man-of-war. The latter vessel put Nicholas ashore at Dartmouth in England, from where he eventually made his way to London. The following July, at Chatham, he joined the crew of the

Berwick. As he then spoke little English, it was impossible for him properly to explain to his crewmates what would happen to him on his rapidly approaching birthday.

The *Berwick* was still anchored at Chatham on 5 August 1709, and Nicholas was overtaken by his trance that morning as he lay in his bunk. When the boatswain could not rouse him, and supposing him to be insubordinately pretending to sleep, he beat him all over with a cane, and when this had no effect, cut down his hammock so that he fell on to the deck. Nicholas lay immobile where he had fallen, completely dead to the world. The boatswain then apprised the ship's lieutenant of his supposed disobedience, and he, with a savagery born of ignorance and arrogance, beat him even harder and for longer. However, far worse treatment was to follow, as his biographer William Hill reveals.

But not thereby awaking him, they call'd the Surgeon of the Ship, who blister'd him all over his Back, then they took a Penknife and cut the Nails of his Fingers from the Flesh, but could not awake him till he came out of his Trance, and then his Body was in so miserable a Condition, by the Barbarity that had been us'd towards him, that he could not stir any of his Limbs for a considerable time after.

Nicholas had previously been troubled by painful kidney stones, and this inhumane treatment not only aggravated the condition but together they rendered him unable to perform his duties aboard ship. He therefore applied for, and was eventually granted, a discharge from the vessel, and was taken ashore and put into St Bartholomew's hospital in West-Smithfield, where he became a patient in Curtain Ward. Two other patients were admitted to the ward at about the same time, one of whom was named William Morgan (*b.* 1680), the other John Palmer (*b.* 1675). Morgan, a disorderly, foul-mouthed, ungodly wretch, was ill with a gangrenous toe, which quickly earned him the sobriquet of 'the man with the sore toe', whereas Palmer, sick with an undisclosed illness, was pleasant, easy-going, and God-fearing, and was soon loved by all.

Nicholas was often visited in hospital by William Hill of Lincoln's Inn, who had heard about his strange entrancements and who took the opportunity to spend many hours talking to him about them. Hill in fact witnessed the trance that overcame him between the 5th and 10th of August, 1710. The following is what Nicholas told Hill about how his out-of-body excursions begin:

When ever he is in any of his Trances, he (as it seems to him) travels a great way on a large sandy beaten Road, having Grass and Fields on both sides of it to his Appearance; which Road he told me, all Souls that leave the body, must and do go, both good and bad; that when they have travelled therein some time, they all come to a great Castle, or Palace, that stands at the end of the Road, in which is heard nothing but great and melodious Rejoycing, Singing, and Ravishing Musick: So that all departed Persons go and knock at the Gate of that Castle, or Palace; that they come thither all naked, only something about their Waste [sic], and all in a great Sweat; that such as hang themselves, or come to untimely Ends, come with a (seeming) Rope about their Necks, and others with the Wounds or Instruments they dy'd by (but these are never let in) that they all knock at the outer Gate for Entrance.

Nicholas Hart thus had no awareness of travelling to the next realm, but rather suddenly found himself walking along the familiar road through green fields to heaven's gate. The road is long and all wraiths march down it clad in nothing but a loin cloth. This seems to verify the ancient belief that all wraiths come naked before the underworld judges. And the 'great Castle, or Palace' is likewise apparently identical to the 'house filled by an ineffable light' entered by Salvius, the 'kind of golden temple' beheld by Turchill, which was distinguished by 'the splendour of its glittering light', and the 'Glorious Mansion' into which went Richard Langly, whose inhabitants were angels and deceased apostles and martyrs.

The gate of heaven, according to Nicholas, had an elderly gate-keeper with cropped white hair and a long white beard.

He wore a top-coat that reached down to his knees, beneath which his legs and his feet were bare. He was particularly distinguished by his astounding knowledge of those who presented themselves before him:

This extraordinary Person knows all the Names and Actions of all that come exactly, and whatever they have done in the Body, and speaks all sorts of Languages; his Voice is so awful and searching, that it quickly pierceth to the Soul and Conscience of those that hear him; that he comes over a Bridge from the Palace or Castle-gate to the outer Gate when any knock to come in, and asks who they are, and what they would have.

Each person then gave his or her name, whereupon the gate-keeper, if they had led lives that were 'good and regular', immediately admitted them, much to their joy and delight. They passed through the gate into a garden full of trees with white flowers, amid the branches of which, and flying from tree to tree like plump birds, were cherubic boys with white curly hair, who were borne aloft by the wings on their backs, and whose round faces beamed welcoming smiles. They also sang lovely anthems to those entering. Some of them picked the white blossoms and strewed them on the walkways, while others made the flowers into garlands and crowns which they placed around the necks or on the heads of the new arrivals. The cherubs, Nicholas learned, were the wraiths of children who died in infancy, and who, while admitted into the first garden of heaven, could go no further. The admitted wraiths did not stay long in the first garden:

And then they pass on through the Walks and Musick, under the Trees, treading on the white Flowers on the Ground, till they pass on through the first Garden into another infinite and endless Place, till they are quite out of sight, and he never sees them more.

The 'infinite and endless Place' is thus the interior of the inner heaven, and one could not hope for a more fitting vista – a possible material emptiness beyond time and space, yet filled, or so we might imagine, with the spirit of God. If so, this explains why the monk of Evesham saw only a bright, wonderful light within heaven's wall, and why those who have had a mystical experience, wherein they achieve union with God, enter what Jan van Ruysbroek (1293–1381) described as 'a wayless abyss of fathomless beatitude' and Meister Eckhart (c.1260–1328) as 'the desert of the Godhead' – or, in other words, into the paradoxical 'nothingness' from which flows everything.

Hence the outer gate or gates, the wall, the palace and the gatekeeper are the last traces of seeming reality, and it is probable that having once passed through the gate into heaven's interior, the purpose of the wraith form is ended and it will gradually dissolve away, thereby releasing the consciousness into a complete and blissful union with the Divinity. Some wraiths, of course, will remain among the encircling paradisial fields and gardens if they are ineligible to enter and are fated to be reborn, but while their existence there is delightful, there is no evidence that it includes the carnal pleasures imagined by Muslims.

Nicholas's regular, once-yearly journeys to heaven's gate meant he became well-known to the elderly gate-keeper.

The ancient Man at the Gate always knows him, calls him by his Name, and every Year lets him into the first Garden of the Palace, where he remains, and about the Palace Gate, till his time comes to return back into this World; and then he calls him, and tells him his time is expir'd, and he must go back again; that then he sighs and sobs (being loath to depart from that joyful Place) and wakes with Trouble.

For no very clear reason, tradition has ascribed the job of gatekeeper to St Peter, the first apostle of Christ, who was crucified at Rome in AD 64. Yet the man described by Nicholas Hart, while he was elderly as Peter was at his death, made no pretension of being the saint, and nor did Nicholas say he was Peter. And while St Peter makes a short appearance in the story of Turchill (see chapter 6), his job, helped by St Paul, was 'to allot to the spirits assembled inside and outside the church the places ordained for them by God according to their desserts'.

When Nicholas was asked if those admitted through heaven's gate ate or drank anything within the castle or palace, and whether night followed day, as in this world,

. . . he smil'd, and said, No, no, no need to eat and drink, and no Night there, but always Light, always Light and Joy, and such Delight as cannot be express'd; and that he saw such things there and without as are not possible to be told with the Tongue of Man; and some things that he must not tell any Creature living . . . I could never get him to declare of what Nature those Secrets were.

As we have noted, Nicholas said the wraiths of those from all countries entered the inner heaven via this gate, and no distinction was made between Protestants, Catholics and those of other Christian churches; however, while the gate-keeper 'did not ask what Opinion any were of that came to the Gate, but how they liv'd, and what good they had done in the World', Nicholas also learned 'that a true Faith in Christ, and a good Life, were the only Means of getting into the Palace' – and that doing good *had* to include being charitable to the poor. If true, it means that non-Christians and atheists are excluded from heaven's interior, although it they have lived good lives they can remain, if only temporarily, in paradise.

What is particularly significant about Nicholas's recovery from his trance on 10 August 1710, which was witnessed by William Hill and others at his bedside, is that after having drunk his customary pints of water, he said that whilst he was at heaven's gate he saw there, applying for entry, first William Morgan and then John Palmer, his two fellow patients in Curtain Ward. Both men in fact had died while Nicholas had lain entranced, but he was not told of this before he disclosed seeing them at the gate. Indeed, Nicholas had only known the former as 'the man with the sore toe', and did not learn his real name until it was spoken by the gate-keeper, which he repeated correctly to those listening. He said that William Morgan was refused entry into ʲeaven, whereas John Palmer, who arrived at the gate shortly before Nicholas had to return to his body and who in fact had died in the morning before he recovered consciousness, was allowed in.

He seriously affirm'd he saw *John Palmer* the Marine afore-said, knock at the Gate of the aforesaid Castle, or Palace, and knew him well, and that he saw him let in presently by the ancient Man, who ask'd him no Questions, but he saw him enter in with great Joy in his Face, his Hands and Eyes being lifted up to Heaven, blessing and praising God, and the little Boys or Angels presently flew with a Crown of Flowers, and put it on his Head, and he saw him walk along the melodious Garden, till he entered into the infinite, endless Place at the end of the first Garden.

The grim fate of William Morgan is related in the next chapter. But clearly, the sighting by Nicholas of the wraiths of both him and John Palmer at heaven's gate, who both died while he lay unconscious in his trance, is a convincing indicator of the genuineness of his experience, and thus of the reality of heaven as he described it. And word about him soon spread, for in September 1710, Nicholas was introduced at St James's Palace to Queen Anne, with whom he spent almost three hours and 'fully satisfied Her Majesty of the Truth of the Matters afore-said, and answer'd what ever Questions Her Majesty and the Persons of Quality put to him in *French*, which he can speak, and *Dutch*, better than *English*'. And we cannot but be impressed by what William Hill wrote of him:

Upon the whole, I really take *Nicholas Hart* to be a very honest serious Fellow, worthy to be believed, and one who durst not be guilty of telling a wilful Lie. I have been divers times, and at divers Places with him alone and in Company . . (I) asked him seriously all the Questions I could think of, and always found him in the same Story . . . I ask'd him if he always in his Trances, went to the same Place, and saw the same Sights; he answer'd yes, but transacted on divers Persons that he knew not; and told me, that the ancient Man at the Gate knew him well, call'd him by his Name, and always let him into the first Garden in the Castle or Palace, where was always ravishing Joys, and melodious Musick, and Singing, and a vast multitude of little Boys, with Wings, flying up and down the Trees.

Although some readers might feel a little uneasy with the image of a 'vast multitude of little Boys, with Wings' flying about among the blossoming trees, their presence, I believe, is adequately explained by them having originated from the souls of dead infants, who had been transformed into cherubs. We also find confirmation of their existence in the experience of the wife of an English naval pensioner, reported in *Present Day Dreams and Visions*, who had an out-of-body experience similar to that of Nicholas Hart. She said:

In the vision I was taken into Heaven and saw two rows of little angels, and then the Son of God, sitting and looking upon them: whilst a great number, whom I thought were my own relations, were standing before Him, in blue Robes. It was so beautiful, and I felt such a heavenly feeling; that I said, I hope I shall be able to stay here, when the Son of God said, 'You cannot stay now, but you shall come, and it will not be long.' Then this great number passed by His right hand, and were gone. I cannot describe the grand sensations I felt at the time of the visions.

An equivalent, if not a greatly superior, number of angels accompanied St Jerome to his meeting with the wraith of Johann Reuchlin. The sleeping Franciscan monk who witnessed their meeting noted, 'The whole Field swarm'd with Myriads of Angels, that flew in the Air as thick as Attomes: If they had not been as clear as the Glass, there would have been no Heaven, nor earth to be seen.'

St Jerome walked with Reuchlin's wraith through the meadow away from the watching monk, and then together they ascended the hill which stood in the middle of it. When they reached its summit a truly breathtaking event happened; it seems that Reuchlin's humanism, particularly his opposition to the German emperor's plan to burn all Jewish books, meant that he received a special welcome in the next world, instead of having to walk along the heavenly road like everyone else.

And now the Heavens open'd, to a prodigious wideness, and there appear'd a Glory so unutterable, as made everything else that pass'd for wonderful before, to look mean, and sordid . . . Out of this Overture, there was let down a great Pillar of fire, which was both Transparent, and very agreeable. By means of this Pillar, Two Holy Souls embracing one another, ascended to Heaven; a Quire of Angels all the while accompanying them, with so charming a melody, that the Franciscan says, he is not able to think of the Delight of it, without weeping.

These several descriptions of the wall of heaven and its paradisial surroundings indicate that there is another, and indescribably wonderful, dimension of being beyond our so-called world of reality, entrance to which is obtained only by the wraiths of those who have lived good lives on earth, although it seems that the gate giving access to heaven's interior is closed to all except Christians. And the sole entrance requirement for them is to have a kind, loving and charitable heart; nothing else has any relevance or importance at all. Indeed, when Nicholas Hart was asked if he would go back to his wealthy father in Holland, who 'had provided well' for his brothers and sisters, he replied: 'I am afraid to be rich, for very few of them are admited into the Palace, in comparison of the poor, afflicted and miserable, in this World.'

And while critics may protest that it is hardly surprising that such a startling claim was made for Christianity because all the NDE returnees considered above were either Christians or came from Christian countries, their objection is only valid if the NDE experiences in question were hallucinatory and thus shaped by the Christian beliefs or upbringing of those who had them. But if the people concerned actually left their bodies and went to where they said they did, then we must either accept their version of what they saw and heard there as true – or believe that they lied about one particular aspect of what was, for each of them, a profound event. We must also note that many pagans, while believing in the existence of paradisial fields and gardens, had no knowledge of the inner heaven described above, which suggests that it was not open to them. But none the less, if Hindu, Buddhist and other eastern mystics can also experience the 'infinite void without beginning' known by some as Nirvana, then why should they not also enter it after death?

When Richard Langly awoke from his coma, during which he had left his body and travelled to paradise, and indeed through that blessed gate, he spoke the following heartfelt words:

That as for the Joys of Heaven, if any Man was sensible of the Happiness which was among the Elected, he would be very cautious of Sinning in this World, for fear of losing the Enjoyment thereof; for in these Blest Bodies was Health without Sickness, Joy without Grief, Ease without Labour, Pleasure without Danger, Comfort without Sorrow, Welfare without Affliction, and Happiness which shall endure to all Eternity.

And the dreadful alternative to heaven, which we call hell, is considered further in the next chapter.

8

Hell Gets Hotter

One undertakes by scales of miles to tell
The bounds, dimensions, and extent of HELL;
How many German leagues that realm contains!
How many cauldrons Hell each year expends
In coals for roasting Huguenots and friends!
From *Satyr IV* by John Oldham

The hell described by early Christians was essentially a combination of the Greek and Jewish underworlds. The Elysian Fields and the Asphodel Fields were brought above ground, and Tartarus was filled with the fire and worms of Gehenna. Hades was dethroned by Jesus and put in chains (possibly along with Persephone), and his place was taken by Satan and his 600 angels-turned-devils. Both old Charon and the three-headed dog Cerberus were dispensed with, although it is possible that Charon may have been re-employed in the 'Pauline' third heaven as the Lake Acherusa boatman. And to emphasize the fact that the demonic new broom swept very dirty, Satan took on a proactive role, using his wiles to lure as many as possible into a life of sin, in order that he might have the pleasure of frying them for eternity. Satan could do this because he was not confined, as he told Bartholomew, in the new underworld, but was free to roam where he willed. For Beliar, as he was formerly and more accurately known, is the Prince of Lies, the Arch Deceiver, the Antichrist. And not only is he still active today but he has just had his best century ever, helped by a liberal and decaying Anglican church.

183

But just as change is a paradoxical constant in the world, so it has likewise affected hell, where the reported conditions worsened considerably before they became somewhat less threatening.

As we have seen, the first accounts of 'the place of torment' or hell portrayed it as a dark, fiery realm, where sinners were either suspended by some part of their anatomy above, or dangled in, fire and brimstone, molten pitch or boiling mud; made to stand in a river of fire and then stabbed, beaten or eaten by worms; or placed in flame-filled pits and individually tortured, or dumped, sometimes minus their hands and feet, in freezing pits.

When Drycthelm of Cunningham in Northumberland had an NDE in AD 693, his wraith was first taken by 'a handsome man in a shining robe' to a terrible landscape where the extremes of heat and cold were used in a unique way to punish sinners:

As we travelled onwards, we came to a very broad and deep valley of infinite length. The side to our left was dreadful with burning flames, while the opposite was equally horrible, with raging hail and bitter snow blowing and driving in all directions. Both sides were filled with men's souls, which seemed to be hurled from one side to the other by the fury of the tempest.

The wraiths confined to that dreadful valley could also leap from side to side, but without finding respite, for the cold was as unbearable as the heat. Yet this awful divide, though a part of hell, was not its worst part, the entrance to which lay at its end (even though it was of 'infinite length') in darkness so intense that Drycthelm, on arriving there with his guide, could see little besides the latter's shining robe.

At that place was a great pit from which came an indescribably foul stench and 'masses of black flame', within which the souls of the damned rose and fell like sparks. This was none other than the foul opening of the inner (or deepest) hell. Drycthelm's guide thereupon vanished, leaving him alone. He watched in impotent horror as five newly condemned wraiths of both sexes were dragged screaming to the pit by laughing devils, who jumped into it with them. Next several 'dark spirits' with glowing eyes and fiery mouths and nostrils sprang from the pit and surrounded Drycthelm. They held a pair of red-hot forceps and threatened to drag him back down into the pit with them, but were stopped by the return of his guide, who appeared behind him on the road along which they had walked in the form of 'what seemed to be a bright star shining in the gloom, which grew in size and came swiftly towards me'.

The guide eventually explained to Drycthelm the difference between the sinners confined to the valley and those thrown or dragged into the pit. The former, it seems, had both confessed their sins and expressed regret for their actions, but not until they were on their deathbeds, which meant that they had to suffer in the valley until the Day of Judgement, when they would be allowed into heaven, although this period could be shortened by the prayers, fasts and almsgiving of the living. Those going into the pit, however, and thus down into the inner hell, were doomed to suffer there eternally, for they were reprobates who had neither confessed their sins nor shown any remorse or regret for their vile acts.

Confirmation of such a dreadful pit is given by the French monk Guibert de Nogent (1053–1124), the Abbot of Nogent-Sous-Coucy, in his autobiography. He says that a pit (although it was not necessarily the same one) was seen by his mother during an out-of-body experience she had while living at Ely convent in England. Madame de Nogent had retired there following the death of her husband Everard, which occurred in the year of Guibert's birth when he fought against the Normans under Duke William, later King William I of England. Guibert relates that one Sunday night in summer after matins his mother fell asleep on the narrow bench in her cell, and underwent a separation from her body.

She thought her spirit left her body without losing her senses. And being drawn, as it were, through a porch, at last issuing from it,

185

she began to come near to the edge of a pit. When close to it, behold from the depths of that pit, people like goblins leapt forth, their hair seeming to be all eaten up with worms, trying to seize her with their hands and to drag her inside.

She was very frightened by this, but before the 'goblins' could make off with her a voice suddenly cried out from behind her, 'Touch her not', which made them jump back into the pit. Then to her astonishment she was joined by the wraith of her late husband:

Being rescued therefore from the dwellers in the pit, and being opposite to the edge thereof, she suddenly saw my father standing by her appearing as he did when a youth . . . Moreover, there was there the figure of a little child crying so bitterly that it troubled her much when she saw it. And being moved by its cries, she said to him, 'How, Lord, can you endure the wailing of this child?' 'Whether I will or not,' said he, 'I endure it.'

The child was there because, when he was alive, Everard had broken his marriage vows and had had an affair with another woman, who became pregnant. But the child died before it could be baptized, so its wraith's continual crying in the nether world was part of Everard's punishment. He informed his wife, however, that he did get some relief from the prayers and masses she said for him.

As we saw in the last chapter, when the consumptive Richard Langly was brought to death's door in 1708, he left his body and was taken to heaven by his angelic guide. But after viewing its delights, he was suddenly transported to either the same or a similar awful pit:

After his Eyes had been ravish'd with the Glorious Sights he saw Above, he thought that in the twinkling of an Eye he was conveyed to the bottomless Pit; in which perpetual Prison of utter Darkness, to his great Terror and dreadful Astonishment, he saw no Order but Horror, no Voice but of Blasphemers and Howlers, no Noise but of

Tortures, no Society but of the Devil and his Angels; who being tormented themselves, wreak'd their Fury on the Damned.

Such a pit is not seen by everybody who is shown hell, and indeed some have found themselves in a gloomy underworld plain which is a counterpart to the paradisial green fields of heaven. This is not surprising as one of the three regions of the Greek nether world was the Asphodel Fields, where languished the wraiths of those who had been neither good nor bad in life.

The plain forming part of the new Christian hell, however, while marshy and muddy underfoot, like parts of the Asphodel Fields, is devoted to more torment and torture than the Greeks could ever have imagined. It is also reached by passage along a 'smooth road'. On this plain the monk of Evesham 'saw and heard crowds of wretched beings collected into miserable troops, and bound in flocks according to the similarity of their crimes and professions', and all were being punished in the most sadistic ways for offences which do not begin to approach the dreadful deeds done, say, by some modern dictators and ethnic cleansers. The monk calls this dark plain the 'first purgatory':

Endless were the kinds of punishment which I saw; some were roasted before fire; others were fried in pans; red hot nails were driven into some of their bones; others were tortured with a horrid stench in baths of pitch and sulphur, mixed with molten lead, brass, and other kinds of metal; immense worms with poisonous teeth gnawed some; others, in thick ranks, were transfixed on stakes with fiery thorns; the torturers tore them with their nails, flogged them with dreadful scourges, and lacerated them in dreadful agonies.

Among those being boiled or fried the monk recognized several former bishops, abbots, judges and others of high-rank, who were 'tormented more than the rest with an increased degree of severity'. This was also true of all who had abused their positions in life to deal harshly or unfairly with people over whom they had jurisdiction.

The monk was afterwards led to the second purgatory, which was a deep valley between two mountains, one side of which was hot and fiery, the other snowy and bitterly cold, so that it was virtually identical to the valley visited by Drycthelm, except that it also contained a black, foetid lake. The punishment therefore involved all three areas, with a regular change around being made: 'Some,' said the monk, 'were tortured by the cold, some by the heat, for a long time, and some were kept for a long period in the stink of the lake'. The lake, by absorbing sinfulness, served to purify those dipped in it, so that the longer a wraith spent in the lake, the better it was for him or her. All wraiths were required to swim or dog-paddle from one end of the lake to the other, the tortures in between becoming milder the closer he or she came to the far end, although 'the lightest torments of that place were more cruel than the most severe ones of the place we saw before'.

The third place of punishment, which lay beyond the two mountains mentioned above, consisted of 'a large plain situated low down in the bosom of the earth'; it was the most traditionally hellish of the three, in the sense of being a combination of Hades and Gehenna, particularly as it was inhabited by ghastly worms:

The surface of that plain was covered by a great and horrible chaos, mixed with a sulphurous smoke, and a cloud of intolerable stench, with a flame of a pitchy blackness, and this rising from all directions was diffused in a dreadful way, through the whole of that void space. The surface of the place abounded with a multitude of worms . . . and these, dreadful beyond conception, of a monstrous size and deformed, with a dreadful gaping of their jaws, and exhaling execrable fire from their nostrils, lacerated the crowds of wretched beings with a voracity not to be escaped from.

The biting and flesh-tearing worms were assisted by devils, who ran wildly through the throng of wraiths, cutting them up into small pieces with their 'fiery prongs', tearing their flesh from the bone, and throwing what was left of them into the surrounding fires. But that was not the end of their suffering because not long afterwards all those so dismembered spontaneously came together again and were made whole, only to find that the whole wretched process was endlessly repeated. The worst punishment, however, was reserved for those who had in life been guilty of a 'wickedness which is unmentionable by a Christian, or even by a heathen or a pagan . . . for till that time I had never heard or thought that both sexes could have been corrupted by such filthiness', which presumably means that they were homosexuals.

Those therefore were continually attacked by huge monsters of a fiery appearance and horrible beyond description, which, notwithstanding their opposition, committed on them the damnable crimes of which they had been guilty on earth; and their cries were horrid until they fainted away apparently dead, when they again revived to be exposed to fresh torments.

It was in this dreadful place that the monk met a lawyer he knew, who had dishonestly enriched himself in life and who was now suffering the consequences. The monk asked the lawyer why he had not helped himself by confessing his sins before he died, and was told that he did confess certain small irregularities to a priest but that his pride prevented him from mentioning the larger ones. He did not, it seems, want it to be known (even by one priest) that he had committed such despicable acts. And apparently, when the monk returned to his body, the priest who had heard the lawyer's confession 'came to me, and called God to witness in the presence of many, that what I said was true, since no one but himself knew these things'.

The Essex peasant farmer Turchill, while essentially a good, God-fearing man, had also not been entirely honest in handing over the correct tithe on his crops, and when he was taken to the vast church at the 'middle of the world', he saw there a

flaming entrance to hell whose fumes made him cough, which
had a reciprocal effect on his comatose body:

Near the [northern] wall was the entrance to the pit of hell, which
incessantly exhaled a smoke of a most foul stench . . . and this
smoke came forth from the tithes unjustly detained, and crops
unjustly tithed; and the stink inflicted incomparable agony on those
who were guilty of this crime. [Turchill] . . . was so oppressed by it
that he was compelled to cough twice, and, as those who stood
round his body declared, his body at the same time coughed twice.

But despite the convenient presence of this smoking pit of hell
no one in the church was thrown into it. The wraiths instead
first had to endure something of an obstacle course, which
took them across country through fire and water to another
church sited on the side of the 'hill of joy', where they were
judged by the apostle Paul and by the devil. It was here that 'a
flame-vomiting aperture, which was the mouth of the pit of
hell, burst out close to the feet of the devil'. Judgement was
reached in the ancient and time-honoured way by using a
scale to weigh the deeds of each person. For this purpose Paul
had two dissimilar weights, both 'shining like gold', while the
pair belonging to the devil were 'sooty and dark'. Those
found to be sinners were then 'hurried away . . .wailing and
cursing the father and mother for having begot it, to eternal
torment, and . . . cast into the deep and fiery furnace, which
was at the feet of the devil who was weighing'.

Much punishment also took place in a large, dark forbidding mansion, somewhat resembling the mother's house in the
film *Psycho*, sited on another mountainside, and which
contained a plethora of chambers, courts and corridors. These
spaces were lined with iron seats on which sinners were held
securely with iron hoops. Both seats and hoops were red-hot
and pierced through with red-hot nails which embedded
themselves in the bodies and limbs of the occupants. This
initial stage of the punishment was therefore similar to that
supposedly meted out to the wraiths in hell witnessed by

190

'Peter', which were suspended by various body parts in flames or boiling pitch, and by 'Paul', which were stood, some up to their eyebrows, in a river of fire. But the dreadful deeds done next were 'sport' for the assembled audience of grinning devils who sat exultantly behind the wailing sinners.

Space does not permit any detailed recitation of the chastisement given to a proud man, a neglectful priest, a murderous soldier, an adulterous couple, two slanderers and some assorted thieves, arsonists, and despoilers of church property, although that imposed on a famous but greedy lawyer who had died not long before Turchill's out-of-body experience should make salutary reading for lawyers everywhere. The man had not only overcharged his clients, but had habitually advised both parties in a case, from whom he had accepted presents in addition to his fee. He was therefore torn from his fiery seat and first made to re-enact his duplicitous, grasping behaviour before the jeering demons. Then he was forced to swallow the red-hot coins which were poured into his outstretched hands. Next a cartwheel with projecting spikes was rotated at speed against his back, tearing away his flesh and splintering his bones. Any burning coins he regurgitated he was forced to pick up and swallow again. Lastly he was torn apart with hooks and prongs by the angry demons, with each grisly portion being thrown into boiling grease and fried, and then he was wholly reconstituted and returned to his red-hot spiked seat until the next time.

The grim mansion also had four courts wherein stood many iron cauldrons. Those in the first, third and fourth courts had furnaces underneath them so that their contents constantly boiled. The cauldrons in the second court held ice and snow, and were thus bitterly cold. The first court cauldrons contained grease and pitch, the third stinking sulphurous water, and those in the fourth court very black and bitter salt water. These cauldrons were the final destination for the wraiths of murderers, sorceresses, robbers and rich men who oppressed their fellows, who were placed in them and boiled or frozen for a time before being shifted around from court to court in the following manner:

191

Those who had been boiling for seven days in [the] burning grease, were on the eighth day plunged into the dreadful cold which was in the second court, whilst those on the other hand who had been tortured in the cold, were put into the burning liquor; in the same way those who had been boiling in the salt water were afterwards tortured in the stench; and they always observed these changes every eight days.

These dreadful scenes were encountered by many others who had NDEs during the Middle Ages and the following centuries, when it was accepted as a matter of course that after death sinners went to hell, where they were destined to suffer the most appalling tortures. The fear of hell was traditionally used as a means of frightening Catholics into doing good and making regular confession of their sins, in order that they were not caught short by sudden death, and to give alms, attend mass, and pray for the wraiths of those who had preceded them. Indeed, every sinner knew that without confession and penitence he or she could not possibly hope ever to go to heaven.

The situation in hell, as reported by those who claimed to have been there, remained unreservedly frightful up to and throughout the seventeenth century. For example, when the Reverend Jeremiah Carter collapsed unconscious on a bridle-path over Warna Scar in December 1630, he was carried away from his comatose body by an angelic guide, first to heaven and then to hell. Of his experiences in the latter dimension, he said:

I beheld a most horrible Place, a bottomless Pit, or a Lake of Fire and Brimstone, out of which came such sulphurous Smoak and Stink, that I was ready to faint; but the Angel comforting me, I began to look farther, where I beheld a Sea overflowing with a Flood of Fire and Brimstone, where I heard the most dismal Cries, Howlings and Yellings; which were fit to melt a Heart of Flint; there I beheld many Thousands of wretched Souls swimming in the Flames, and the Devil tormenting them with all manner of Cruelties.

The sinners selected for such additional cruel treatment were swearers and blasphemers, perjurers, scoffers at religion and despisers of God's word, the proud, 'which,' he adds, 'are the first rank', gluttons and drunkards, misers, oppressors of the poor, and two groups who are commonly encountered today. 'Here were Gallants that took Delight in nothing but the Pleasures of the World, as Ranting, Roaring, Singing, Whoring, Carding and Dicing, whose Souls were as horribly tormented with all Sorts of Miseries, as they took Delight in all Sorts of Pastimes. There were the Envious and Discontented, howling like mad Dogs.'

When the English Civil War broke out between King and Parliament a few years later, such torments were naturally expected to be suffered by deceased traitors and enemies. One royalist who notably raised the ire of parliamentarians in 1645 was Sir Peter Ball, a commissioner for Exeter, who was caricatured in hell, where he was supposedly seen by a Devon boy named Joseph Buxton, a survivor of the Cavaliers' defeat at Langport in Somersetshire on 10 July. The devil himself, wrote the anonymous author of the pamphlet describing the event, specifically carried young Buxton to hell to witness the agonies of poor Sir Peter, who had lately died: 'His Legs and Feet [were] scorching in furious flames, his Buttocks upon a Grediron, his Back and Shoulders in a frying pan, his Head in a boiling kettle of pitch, bellowing and roaring out in grievous sort, and cursing the hour of his nativity, with his extorting, covetousness, and cheating of the Country.'

Joseph Buxton also saw the preparations being made for the arrival of the wraiths of George, Lord Goring, the former governor of Portsmouth, who had commanded the Cavaliers at Langport (and who did not die until 1658), and of his right-hand-man Sir Richard Greenville, both of whom were due to have four ladles of scalding aconite dispatched down their throats!

When Nicholas Hart had his annual five-day trance in 1710, he also saw sinners being taken to hell, although their dispatch thither was different from that reported by visitants

193

in earlier years. For example, the elderly gatekeeper alone decided who came into heaven and who went to hell. It was his knowledge of each wraith's identity and what he or she had done in life which enabled him to do this. The sinners, moreover, were collected from the gate by Satan himself, who delivered them directly to the pit of hell, which lay close by the left-hand side of the heavenly gate. Those taken off were a similar rabble of liars, drunkards, gluttons, swearers, whore-mongers, misers, the greedy and the unmerciful, who were seen suffering in hell by Jeremiah Carter. Their pick-up was a dramatic moment.

Satan presently appears at the Gate in the Shape of a black Man, with a Cart or Carr (as appeared to him), which is drawn by two black Dogs, with black curl'd Tails, their Claws being about a Foot long, and he lays hold of all them that are deny'd Entrance into the Castle or Palace, and throws them into the Carr, sometimes twenty at a time, and drives them away (they shrieking, roaring and yelling all the time, in a most terrible and inexpressible manner) to a great dark Hole or Pit hard by . . . and casts them in roaring and yelling, where they fall down a long while, till they are out of sight.

In the last chapter I mentioned that Nicholas recognized the wraith of William Morgan, 'the man with the sore toe', when Morgan arrived at the gate, and heard the gatekeeper call out his name, which Nicholas did not know before then. Morgan was told he had been 'always a wicked Man' who had failed to heed the 'good Instructions' of his parents, and that he must therefore go to hell. And indeed not long afterwards Satan arrived with his dog-cart, threw Morgan and several other screaming wretches into it, and carried them off without further ado.

William Hill, Nicholas Hart's biographer, recollects:

He further told me, that there are two Carrs drawn and drove as aforesaid, and that one comes every Minute to the Gate, to carry away those that are deny'd Entrance to the Palace: that very few

enter therein in comparison of those that are driven away in the
Carrs . . . and that some come every Minute of an Hour from all
Parts of the World.

If one cart left heaven's gate every minute with twenty wraiths
aboard, a total of 1,200 sinners could be dispatched to hell
each hour, or 28,800 a day, a figure which is surprisingly close
to the 30,000 daily deaths supposedly revealed by Jesus to
Bartholomew, fifty-three of which were allowed into heaven.
Yet we are told 'sometimes twenty at a time' were sent to hell
every minute, which means that the number was usually less
than that. If the average had been ten per minute, then 14,400
wraiths would have been sent daily to hell, or 5,256,000
during 1710. As about 1 per cent of the population die each
year, the total world population in 1710, using these figures,
would therefore have been about 526 million. This is remarkably close to the estimated total of 550 million.

However, the population of the world has now risen to
about 6.2 billion. This huge number will generate around
170,000 wraiths arriving daily at heaven's gate, or 7,083 per
hour. Hence if Satan still has only two dog-carts to ship the
vast bulk of these off to hell, and if he packs twenty wraiths
into each cart, he and his fellow driver will *both* have to make
a return journey every 20 seconds to keep up. So perhaps even
Satan is badly stressed nowadays, although the different rate
at which time passes in the next world may help him cope!

The wraith of Mary Stone, the Kent farmer's daughter, had
a similar excursion into the next world during her NDE.
Taken first through some 'very pleasant green fields' by her
guide, she was afterwards escorted to the border of Satan's
domain:

We came in sight of the dismallest place sure that ever was, where
I heard the most dismal cries and groans, and smelt the most
nauseous stink of fire and brimstone, that no tongue can express
the dismal cries of the one, and the nauseous smell of the other,
which put me in a great fright: my guide bid me not be dismayed,

for no harm should come unto me. I asked him what dismal place
that was? He said unto me, that is the place called HELL, which the
wicked are sent to after death.

But although Mary mentioned the stench of fire and brimstone and the 'dismal cries and groans' of those lodged there,
she apparently saw no flickering flames or devils or wraiths
being horribly tortured. Indeed, if we substitute a 'foetid
smell' for that of the traditional fire and brimstone, Mary
could be describing a walk past London's Newgate gaol,
where the same sense of forlorn hopelessness existed among
the inmates.

A similar milder view of hell was revealed to Henry Webb
not long after he had been denied entry into heaven, as
described in chapter 6. For Henry, having been apprised of his
sinfulness, kept begging those at the gate to change their
minds, until at last one of the 'men in bright clothes' told him
to look to his left.

Which he doing, saw at some distance from him, hell itself
opened, which seemed covered with the most dismal, lonesome,
and doleful darkness it is possible to imagine, and sent forth a
suffocating smell of sulphur; but he did not discern any flames: he
saw a great multitude of persons in it, seemingly in the utmost
agonies and torments, and the prince of darkness, as it were,
raging as a ravenous lion to come at him: but what struck him with
still more horror and despair, was to distinguish the faces of three
of his old wicked companions among those tormented wretches, as
plain as he ever saw any persons with his eyes.

Henry gazed at this scene for what seemed to him to be
several hours, struck dumb by its awfulness and by the fact
that his sins had condemned him to go there. But upon at last
finding his voice, he begged the man in shining clothes to be
allowed to return to his body in order to 'have some time to
repent of and reform his wicked life'. The angel replied only
that he was going to hell, which made Henry beseech him

'more vehemently' for a second chance, until at last he was told that he could return to life for a few months, during which time he had to amend his ways completely or suffer the consequences. The man in shining clothes then walked with Henry for a distance of some 2 or 3 miles from the gate of heaven, all the while upbraiding him for his sinful ways and warning him that unless he wholly changed 'the torment he had seen would be his for ever and ever'.

After the departure of this glorious person from him, he seemed to travel for many miles through places dark, desolate, horrible, beyond all that tongue or pen can express, being at the same time grievously oppressed with this heavy burden of his sins, which seemed to be all before his eyes, set against him in terrible array. He cannot describe in what manner he returned to life, but is informed that some of the people below stairs, hearing a deep groan, came up to the room, and found life coming into him.

Henry Webb's experience is of course similar to Nicholas Hart's in that both men walked unaccompanied in their disembodied state to heaven's gate and, upon reaching it, were made aware that the entrance to hell lay somewhere off to the left, although hell opened to reveal its interior for Henry but not for Nicholas. And the opened hell was primarily a place of darkness, without flames and burning, even though the smell of brimstone (or sulphur) was still evident, as were numerous sinners. However, the latter were only 'seemingly in the utmost agonies and torments', which suggests that while they were crying out and groaning in much the same manner as Mary Stone had heard, they were not necessarily being physically tortured.

In his book *A Discourse on Dreams and Night-Visions*, published in 1791, the Reverend David Simpson (1745–99) relates the remarkable experience of hell that a hackney coachman had in a dream one Saturday night 'not long since', which naturally places it towards the end of the eighteenth century. We have noted that a person's double is able to leave his or her body during sleep, when whatever is then seen, heard or experienced is often mistaken for an ordinary dream on awakening. In his dream the coachman found himself out driving in his coach, which was booked for hire by some people who directed him to drive first up, then down the other side of, a very steep hill, at the bottom of which were

. . . a pair of great iron gates, wide open. When he had passed them, he found himself in an uncommonly dark and gloomy place, in which were vast crowds of people dressed in mourning, all of whom, by their countenances, seemed to be in a very pensive frame of mind. Hereupon he stopped, and asked one of the persons, what place that was? He answered, It was hell.

The coachman expressed surprise at this, saying that he thought hell would have been far more frightening and adding that he would not be nearly so fearful of the place thereafter.

Upon this the person informed him, that hell was not so much outward, as it was inward; and, as a proof of this, he opened his waistcoat and showed him his heart, which was in a flame of fire. This shocked the coachman to a great degree: but the person proceeded to inform him, that his case was not singularly shocking; for all whom he then saw were in the same condition.

The man then offered to show him many others in a worse state than himself, whereupon the alarmed coachman attempted to leave. However, he was forcibly restrained by that inmate and several others, who told him that he would not be allowed to go unless he agreed to return the following day at noon. After vainly struggling to free himself, the coachman at last promised to come back, whereupon he woke up in bed, horrified by what had taken place. He recounted the dream to his wife, 'but she treated it with ridicule' and went back to sleep.

The following day the coachman refused to go to work and begged his wife to find someone to take his place, but she only complained of his foolishness to a friend, ridiculing his fear of dying at noon. Yet when noon struck and she taunted him for not having gone to hell, he cried out, 'Hold your tongue, for I am going,' and immediately dropped down dead!

This is one of the few accounts in which we find hell being entered, like the Greek Tartarus and other pagan nether worlds, via a gate rather than a pit. Yet in the *Divine Comedy*, the Italian poet Dante (1265–1321) describes himself being escorted into hell (an event which supposedly happened in 1300), by the wraith of the Roman poet Virgil, through a gate upon whose 'lofty arch' were inscribed the now-famous words:

> Through me you pass into the city of woe:
> Through me you pass into eternal pain:
> Through me among the people lost for aye,
> Justice the founder of my fabric moved:
> To rear me was the task of power divine,
> Supremest wisdom, and primeval love.
> Before me things create were none, save things
> Eternal, and eternal I endure.
> All hope abandon, ye who enter here.

Virgil, the author of the epic poem the *Aeneid*, was chosen by Dante to be his fictitious guide because he had described the descent of his hero Aeneas into Hades, who went there to look again upon the face of his dead father. Aeneas' guide was not Mercury, but the Sibyl, a prophetic wise-woman, who resided in a cave at Cumae in Italy.

The difference between the hell perceived by Richard Langly in the first decade of the eighteenth century and that of the hackney coachman, albeit in a dream, in about 1790 is considerable. Langly's hell is still the dark, fiery torture-chamber witnessed by visitants of the previous century and earlier, whereas the coachman's, while dark and forbidding, lacks flame, brimstone and 'physical' torment, the suffering of its inmates arising from within themselves, of which the burning heart is perhaps a symbol, and which presumably comes from an understanding of the effects of their actions on their victims. Hence they are locked up with other sinners in a dreary enclosure with nothing but their consciences.

Not long afterwards, however, in 1801, the anonymous young woman mentioned in chapter 5 had an NDE in Swansea. She described what transpired in verse, including a visit first to the opening and then to the depths of hell. But while hell's principal feature initially seemed to be darkness, she later discovered that the wraiths confined to it are being tortured:

> But, oh! My friends, I tremble while I tell,
> Aghast I stood upon the mouth of hell;
> Transfix'd with horror, I the gulf survey'd,
> At which my soul was dreadfully dismay'd;
> Seven-fold darkness was beneath my feet,
> On either side, nought else my eye could meet.
> Wild with despair, I upward turn'd my eyes,
> And saw a lid of a tremendous size
> Hang o'er my head, just ready for to close
> To sink my soul in everlasting woes;

Just then, God saved her from being shut in and told her that she could return to earth and her body. However, before being whisked completely away, God decided that a direct experience of hell would be of benefit to her:

> My soul descended then as quick as thought,
> And into hell's interior I was brought.
> There I beheld the souls of wicked men,
> Writhing in torture in this horrid den . . .
>
> One above all appear'd to my surprise,
> His tongue was parch'd – he roll'd his tortur'd eyes;
> His awful pain was great beyond degree,
> He seem'd to me in dreadful agony.

[God then speaks to her again]
He said, 'That soul you see tormented so,
In Swansea died but a few days ago!'
His name He told me, which I knew quite well,
But never thought to see his soul in hell.
Harden'd he died, while in the trance I lay,
And in hell's torments he is doom'd to stay.

If we can accept this description as accurate – and the writer of the preface to her poem states that 'It is not a flight of fancy, or an idle tale; its contents are facts, plainly stated, without exaggeration' – her experience shows that although hell could sometimes manifest in the form of psychological torment, the use of torture did not stop.

Not long after she recovered from her illness, she married a soldier in the 49th Foot Regiment, commanded by General (later Sir) Isaac Brock (1769–1812), and in 1802 went with them to Canada. She was separated from her husband Robert for a year when he was imprisoned with 40 other British troops by the Americans following their capture of Fort George, Upper Canada, in 1813. They afterwards spent an adventurous life together, which included residence in a log cabin and fighting with Indians in America. She also gave birth to five more children, making seven in all, although none survived childhood. But her roving ended with the death of Robert from illness, when she returned to Britain. She did not publish her poetical account of her NDE and of her North American experiences until 1826, when she was forty-seven years old.

About 5 per cent of those who have a near-death experience today find themselves in a negative or distressing environment similar to that 'dreamed' by the eighteenth century hackney coachman. The commonest scene is indeed a pitch-dark place inhabited by numerous wraiths whose demeanour bespeaks depression and hopelessness: they have slumped shoulders and bowed heads, vacant or mournful expressions and down-cast, empty eyes, and they shuffle aimlessly around. They speak neither to one another nor, indeed, to the person newly arrived among them. Their clothes are either black or a dirty white, while their colour is often grey.

When a young American woman named Angie Fenimore, the author of *My Near-Death Journey to the Edge of Hell*, tried to commit suicide by slitting her wrists and swallowing prescription medicines, she lost consciousness and left her body. She visited two dark places in her out-of-body state. The first was 'an endless void' without light, which was inhabited by morose and non-communicative teenagers, all of whom wore black clothes of a modern style. They had no interest in either her or each other, and she realized that they were the wraiths of suicides.

Then rising rapidly upwards, Angie came to a second place, a 'shadowy plane' whose surface, while supportive, was covered in a swirling waist-high black mist. She realised she was in 'a state of Hell, but this was not the typical "fire and brimstone" Hell that I had learned about as a child. The word *Purgatory* rose, whispered, into my mind'. Strangely, she could discern various items of antique American furniture standing in the mist, which appeared to be less solid than objects in this world, but none the less 'far more real'. The plane was also populated by suicide victims, but these were adults, of a range of ages, and who all emanated a dark aura. They wore dirty white robes. She realized that many had been there for a very long time. No one spoke, but Angie was able telepathically to read their thoughts. Some were entirely self-absorbed, trying endlessly to justify what they had done, whereas others had given up thinking completely. All were lonely in the crowd.

This dismal scene helps explain why recovered suicide victims invariably say their attempt to kill themselves solved nothing and only landed them in a far worse situation. Life, it seems, is not only a gift, but a gift with a serious purpose, which is to allow the conscious double form to experience and learn from the environment into which the temporary home of its physical self is born, and from the ups and down of existence to which he or she is exposed. Hence anyone jumping ship by committing suicide prematurely breaks his or her chain of lives and can no longer progress any further, which is why they find themselves in death's dark junk yard, without anything, even hope.

Yet oddly Dante pictured suicides as residing in the seventh gulf or circle of hell, into which each of their wraiths help-lessly descended as a seed into the dark forest grown from its predecessors:

> . . . into the wood it falls,
> No place assign'd, but wheresoever chance
> Hurls it; there sprouting, as a grain of spelt,
> It rises to a sapling, growing thence
> A savage plant. The Harpies, on its leaves
> Then feeding, cause both pain, and for the pain
> A vent to grief.

However, as Dante listened to a tree so formed lament its past foolishness, he saw two naked wraiths being chased through the forest by black mastiff dogs. He recognised both: one was a citizen of Padua named Sant' Andrea, the other a Sienesse named Lano, whose prodigality had ruined them and driven them to suicide. Dante could only watch in horror as the huge dogs caught them and tore them into pieces, and then ran off with their limbs.

Dante's *Divine Comedy* is also unusual in representing hell as still giving work to Charon and Cerberus. The old boat-man, however, no longer rowed wraiths across the river Styx, but over its tributary, the Acheron, while Cerberus had been retired from gate watching and now kept his three pairs of canine eyes on the gluttonous sinners kept in the third circle of hell, at whom he barked furiously and then ripped them apart. Even more surprisingly, Dante's hell had another ferry-man, whom the poet calls Phlegyras. He rowed wraiths across the Stygian lake to the so-called city of Dis (whose name is taken from the old Roman god of the dead), which was the region's counterpart to the city of Christ. Dis had iron walls and its interior was 'thick spread with sepulchres' containing the wraiths of heretics, which were being baked like buns in an oven by the surrounding flames!

But while those sent to hell do occasionally get the chance to be helped by wraiths undergoing an NDE, like that of Angie Fenimore – or Heracles, for that matter – they rarely take advantage of such direct assistance. Indeed, when Bloynan visited hell during his two-and-a-half day coma in St Thomas's Hospital (see chapter 6), he tried to perform such a supernatural rescue for an acquaintance he met there, only to discover that the man concerned would not make any effort to help himself.

The drama happened when Bloynan's wraith arrived in a barren landscape, which was, he said, 'in permanent gloom ' and which he surmised was hell. The milieu was one of endless frustration and anxiety. While its sky lacked any sun, moon or stars, the ground gave out a dim light, providing a visibility of about 200 yards. In the murkiness Bloynan saw a man he recognized, whom he had known and disliked in life and whose character was unpleasant and sadistic. Yet this individual did not seem to recognize him.

He was sitting on a rock surrounded by a pool of his own malice like a bad smell, which extended about four metres around him. He carried this with him at all times wherever he went. I had the task of making a cart to transport him out of there. This was impossible in practice. The only materials available were two tree trunks about a metre in diameter, from which the wheels were to be cut, and two lengths of wood for the struts. But no saw or others tools were available. And he wouldn't help me. He simply sat on the rock expecting that I should produce a vehicle without any assistance or communication from him. So I thought, 'If that's your attitude, you can do it yourself', and left him there.

Bloynan realized the man was beyond help, which probably meant that his own failings, weaknesses and malevolence were condemning him to remain on that rock indefinitely. It was about such personal entrapment that Swedenborg pertinently wrote:

All man's will and love remains with him after death. He who wills and loves evil in the world, wills and loves the same evil in the other life, and then he no longer suffers himself to be withdrawn from it. This is the reason that a man who is in evil is bound to hell, and is actually there as to his spirit; and after death desires nothing more than to be where his evil is; consequently man after death casts himself into hell, and not the Lord.

Yet as we have seen, those condemned to hell or to any of its peripheral regions can be aided by prayer, by the intercession of angels and saints (whose assistance is prompted by prayer), by Catholic masses, and apparently by almsgiving, all of which can lessen the torment inflicted, shorten eternity to a measurable span, give comfort and prompt hope. The latter is particularly important to those poor souls like suicides who are lost in darkness and despair.

9

Imagination or Reality?

How can it enter into the thoughts of man, that the soul, which is capable of such immense perfections, and of receiving new improvements to all eternity, shall fall away into nothing almost as soon as it is created?

From the *Spectator*, No. 111

We have now examined many accounts of heaven and hell, which were related by, or for, those who claimed to have visited them. Their reportage has given us some wonderful revelations of the former and some dreadful insights into the latter. But did they really go there or were they deceived by their own imaginary constructs?

The existence of the next world is predicated upon the supposition that the human body contains something which survives its death. You cannot in fact have one without the other. I have postulated that what survives our physical self is our consciousness enclosed within our double form, which together constitute the wraith. The double thereby provides consciousness with a lodgement wherein it can function in ways that are familiar to it. And indeed, the number of sightings of doubles and wraiths from all parts of the world and in all ages suggests that they are a reality. This in turn means that existence in the next world, at least in the short term, resembles life here. Wraiths therefore interact with each other as living people do, and they perceive and experience their surroundings in the same way.

207

The latter point is affirmed by Emanuel Swedenborg, who claimed to have frequently seen and interacted with a number of the next world's inhabitants. After noting in *Heaven and Hell* that a person's spirit or wraith initially has the same appearance as its physical self, he goes on to say:

A man as a spirit also enjoys every sense both external and internal which he enjoyed in the world; he sees as before; he hears and speaks as before; he smells and tastes as before, and, when he is touched, he feels as before; he also longs, desires, wishes, thinks, reflects, is affected, loves, and wills, as before; and he who is delighted with studies, reads and writes as before.

Swedenborg's observations are supported by those next-world visitants described in this book, all of whom found themselves in their familiar bodily form, and who walked around, took in their surroundings, and talked with others as they had done in life. But Swedenborg also says that wraiths in heaven have better eyesight and hearing.

They who are in heaven perceive, that is, they see and hear more exquisitely, and also think more wisely than when they were in the world; for they see from the light of heaven, which exceeds, by many degrees, the light of the world; and they hear by a spiritual atmosphere, which likewise exceeds, by many degrees, the atmosphere of the earth.

Such improved visual and auditory capabilities have also been reported by many recent returnees. But while wonderful odours are sometimes also experienced, there is seldom any betterment of the senses of taste and touch.

Some communication, however, takes place by telepathy, although this is rarely as noticeable and as all-encompassing as that experienced by Bloynan. Swedenborg relates how when he was once brought to the brink of death, the two angels who came to sit by his head, while remaining silent, did pass on their thoughts to him. He says they achieved this 'by looking into my face . . . for in this manner communication of thought is effected in heaven'.

Furthermore, if the wraith is quasi-physical, by which I mean it possesses some properties in common with the matter of this world, we would expect it to be transported to a region or dimension made out of the same stuff. This in fact is not only suggested by the many out-of-body experiences I have related, but is directly referred to by Angie Fenimore, who visited the dark, negative plane inhabited by the wraiths of suicide victims where she found, in comparison with our world, 'things seemed less solid though they were far more real, indestructible'.

The next world consists of two dissimilar regions, one of which is distinguished by its light, the other by its darkness, a difference which has been reported time and again by those who have had NDEs, some of whom visited the light place, some the dark place, and some both. The outer region of light has a landscape of stunning beauty and fruitfulness, and is suffused with such positive emotions as love, joy and hope. The landscape of the dark region is ugly and barren, and is redolent with hatred, despair, and hopelessness. The former, which we call heaven, is the post-mortem destination of many of those who lived open, loving lives, some of whom will enter its inner region, while the latter, which we call hell, is inhabited by the wraiths of people who lived selfishly and dishonestly.

This twofold division of wraiths into those who are rewarded in heaven and those who are punished in hell means we live in a moral universe. Hence our actions while alive *are* held to account after death and we are judged accordingly.

Although heaven has been placed somewhere up in the sky and hell below ground for most of the last two thousand years, there was a lot of initial uncertainty about where exactly the good went after death. For while most early Christians thought it was to heaven, some believed heaven was situated, like the Elysian Fields, below ground, and others that it was found on western islands lying somewhere beyond the Ocean Stream. Only later was it decided that heaven was really in the aerial 'third heaven', and thus in the sky. The third heaven was then credited with having within its borders an inner region or 'city of Christ', entry into which was reserved for good Christians alone and which therefore became for them heaven proper.

It is easy to criticize such uncertainty as arising from the massaging of ancient pagan Greek and Jewish beliefs to suit Christian ideology, but we could equally well argue that because knowledge of the next world comes from occasional and unexpected visits made there, it naturally took time to build up a picture of what the beyond is really like. But how do we explain the so-called city of Christ, which is off-limits to everybody except Christians? Did nobody pass through its gate until after the resurrection? This might have been the case if there was actually then no gate for them to enter, although as we have seen the underworld of the ancients was certainly believed to have a gate. But none the less, it is still possible that God, following Christ's crucifixion, created a special gate opening into the inner heaven for good Chrstians. A similar difficulty applies to the next world *per se*. When exactly did it come into existence? As paradise appears to contain, with the exception of the odd horse and dog, the wraiths of only *Homo sapiens*, does its genesis date from the origin of our species? But if some dogs and horses make it there, why not all canines and equines and indeed all animal life? We also know that both paradise and the area directly within heaven's gate are reportedly home to a variety of plants. But is such vegetation indigenous to those places or is it formed from the wraiths of plants that once grew on earth? Dante ingeniously suggests that the trees growing in hell were formerly vicious people, which if true would certainly reflect the mental capacity of many criminals. We have no clear answers to these questions, and can only wait for more information.

The wraiths which have from time to time been seen rising upwards, often borne aloft by angels, after bodily death, support the notion of an aerial heaven, as do the accounts of those NDE returnees who said they were either carried up into, or found themselves in, the sky or even space. Yet confusingly, the majority of wraiths are not carried away in this manner. Most are met by a guide who then walks with them to heaven and then to hell, or vice versa, while others make their own way around. But the ability to walk between heaven and hell is frequently recorded, and indeed hell has a recognizable landscape consisting of valleys, mountains, rivers and lakes, which are aflame, freezing or putrid. This landscape is therefore the reverse or opposite of heaven's paradisial fields and gardens. It also has dark buildings wherein nightmarish punishments occur. Beneath the dreadful countryside lies the inner hell, access to which is by pits emitting a ghastly stench and black flames. One pit even lies a short distance from heaven's gate.

Such is the apparent basic geography of the next world. But how does it align itself with ours?

Although certainty is impossible, the evidence I have gathered seems to suggest that paradise and hell lie on the same quasi-physical plane or surface, the overall shape of the former, according to Swedenborg, being that of a man, while that of the latter is of a demon. This plane apparently intersects the physical sphere of our planet, the heavenly end or half projecting into the sky, the opposite half bearing hell therefore lying underground, and thus in both the dark and, further down, in continual fire. Indeed, should this intersecting plane be circular and have a diameter greater than that of the earth, it would produce a paradisial ring or halo around our planet resembling the physical rings of Saturn. Either arrangement has a symbolic aptness because those descending to a hell placed within the earth do so because they love the world and material things, while those rising above to heaven do so because they have scant regard for the world and its vanities, and seek spiritual things.

Such an arrangement effectively explains some of the various oddities mentioned by different NDE returnees, although we must remember that while the plane passes through our material dimension, it does not touch it in the accepted sense of the word, and it cannot, in normal circumstances, be seen or otherwise experienced. This is why no pilot has ever (to my knowledge at least) flown into heaven and no miner dug his way down to hell. And if there really is a pit located close by the heavenly gate, then this must in fact be the opening of a large tunnel which curves under the heavenly surface and thus down into the underside of the landscape of hell. The plane has its own gravity and is not affected by that of the earth.

The rivers, gardens, fields and buildings of paradise, and the wall and gate of, and buildings within, the inner heaven, and also the pits, chambers, mansions and even instruments of torture of hell, being composed of the same quasi-physical or spiritual 'substance' as wraiths, will ordinarily be experienced by them as tangible landscapes or objects with their own characteristic qualities of brightness or darkness. However, if the heavenly region remains invisible to some wraiths, as most doubles and wraiths do to us, then they will find themselves apparently floating in space and looking down at the earth below and at the moon and the stars of our dimension, as happened to Fursey, Salvius and Carl Jung. And it is possible that if the same thing happened in the hellish region, they would find themselves entirely surrounded by molten rock.

Any wraith seen by living observers being carried up into the sky by angels, as was the abbess Hilda, would normally appear to itself, one suspects, to be transported over the landscape of paradise. And a wraith being taken to hell may either experience its journey as a descent into the bowels of the earth or alternatively as an entry into a dark, forbidding landscape above which rises a sky without a sun, moon or stars, such as happened, for example, to Drycthelm and the monk of Evesham.

The punishment a wraith receives in hell depends upon the nature of the person's life. All the newly dead, it seems, are shown some type of review or playback of their lives and are thus brought face to face with any wrongs they have done – by which is meant, in essence, the pain, hurt and distress that they have caused to others. Thereafter some will find themselves in the abyssal darkness of the earth's interior, where they may also be exposed to the heat of its core. This would naturally account for the traditional belief in, and frequent witnessing of, hell fire, although it is probable that the fires of hell exist only in the other-world dimension. As we have noted, one of the angelic guides that carried the wraith of Fursey into the sky told him: 'Every man's body is consumed by unlawful desire, and when death frees him from his body, he must make due atonement for his sins by fire.' And Fursey's wraith was burned on its shoulder and jaw for a minor misdemeanour when a sinner, who was being held in some aerial flames, was thrust against him. The wound was transferred to his physical body when he returned to it.

And despite the testimony of Nicholas Hart and others, Swedenborg believed that sinners naturally direct themselves to hell, for it emits a compelling odour of lust, deceit, riot and self-interest, things which they found so attractive in life. They are heartily welcomed by devils when they first arrive, but are then afflicted with unspecified 'cruel punishments' and reduced to a state of slavery. However, much of the horror of hell, he says, derives from the constant state of turmoil that exists there, which is caused by the same hatred, suspicion and desire to succeed at all costs that formerly motivated its inhabitants. It is this, he intriguingly suggests, that symbolizes hell fire.

But as rebellious commotions are of continual occurrence there, because every one desires to be the greatest, and burns with hatred against others, new insurrections are made, thus one scene is changed into another, and they who were made slaves are delivered, that they may assist some new devil to subjugate others . . . Such torments are the torments of hell, which are called hell fire.

But none the less, we cannot escape the fact that many visitants to hell have witnessed dreadful forms of torture being carried out, apart from that of burning. Such direct, active punishment was claimed for the pagan underworld, although as we have seen the chastisement carried out in hell became increasingly violent and sadistic until the eighteenth century, when the spread of science and rationality seemingly went hand-in-hand with its diminution. Indeed, since then it has become more usual for visitants to hell to find that its inhabitants endure essentially the same torment they once inflicted on others. But this is not physically inflicted; rather, it comes from an understanding of the suffering they caused, which brings them reciprocal anguish and which may even ignite their hearts!

It is too easy and convenient, however, to say that hell has no torments such as those once described for it, and to dismiss them as the sadistic fantasies of disturbed individuals. Wraiths, after all, have the same sensations as the living, and can feel pain and discomfort. Why would they have kept these if they are not used? But God, we are constantly told, loves us and would not countenance such horrors. God, however, does not reign in hell, for as the novelist Henry Fielding, echoing the opinion of the day, once sagely remarked, the 'absolute power in his infernal dominions is granted to their diabolical ruler'. Thus Satan governs hell, he chooses the punishments, and those who go there have only themselves to blame.

Moreover, Christ himself in the parable of Lazarus and the rich man portrays the latter as burning in hell. He also speaks of the fire and worms of Gehenna, which await sinners. Indeed, Jesus' love for mankind was expressed as a readiness to forgive sin, but those who break God's laws and who neither repent nor ask for forgiveness can expect no mercy. We must also remember that the natural world, while of almost paradisial beauty, is an environment of constant struggle, pain, anguish and death for the creatures that inhabit it. No one blames God for such misery, as it is regarded as a concomitant of life, just as fire and torture are seemingly a concomitant of hell. But we, as rational beings, have the ability to make choices, and those who deliberately put themselves before others cannot complain if they end up there.

Each person is responsible for his or her actions, and there are no liberal lawyers waiting to help sinners out.

Morality is therefore the God-given measure of human behaviour. Its basis is simple and entirely straightforward: all that we do which is harmful to others is sinful, while that which helps others is good. Thus selfishness is the root of sin, for it generates hatred, malice and greed, whereas selflessness, from which flows love, pity and concern, is the way of right-eousness, or the prime good. And Satan, busy as he is at heaven's gate, does not need to spend time tempting us for our natural greed does his work for him. This is why the numbers admitted to hell vastly exceed those going to heaven.

The critics of the NDE invariably argue that the people concerned were not really dead and that their next world excursions are visual and auditory hallucinations. Yet ironi-cally, such quibblers are often the very same people who argue in favour of organ transplantation, which is based on the supposition that a patient certified as 'brain dead' is dead, even though they know that every other part of his or her body is very much alive. Indeed, donated organs must be living. Hence to claim that someone whose heart and breathing have stopped is not dead if he or she is later resuscitated, whereas a person whose heart and breathing have not stopped at all is dead, is nothing more than a wicked piece of double-think.

But while many people throughout the ages have appar-ently left their bodies in their wraith form and visited heaven and/or hell, their accounts of what these places are like are often quite different. I have already explained that such differ-ences will certainly occur if the landscapes of heaven and of hell are extensive and varied, for dissimilar scenes will be encountered depending upon which part an individual wraith is taken to or sent. None the less, these varieties of scene have prompted some modern critics to claim that the witnessed landscapes are hallucinations caused either by a lack of oxygen or by administered drugs. Hence their origin, if this is true, really lies in the subject's own psychology and in his or her afterlife expectations, if any.

In this respect it is relevant to note that many of the NDE cases I have examined occurred in earlier times, and several have not seen the light of day since they were first printed. They therefore pre-date Raymond Moody's book *Life After Life* by many years and are entirely free of its influence. This may explain why none of the people concerned reported leaving their bodies and travelling down a tunnel towards a bright light or talking with an entity Moody calls the 'being of light'. Yet they all enjoyed 'enhanced cognitive functioning' in the form of clearer and faster thoughts and brighter and more vivid perceptions.

More importantly, none of them was given modern drugs which might have prompted hallucinations. Hence with the exception of the very early Greek cases, in which an NDE may have been initiated by the eating of plant poisons, their remarkable experiences were not induced by opiates, pain killers or anaesthetics. In any case, as Susan Blackmore says in an article published in the *Journal of the Royal Society of Medicine*, 'Research shows that patients given anaesthetics or pain-killers have fewer, or more muted and less detailed, NDEs than others.' It is likewise true that their experiences are unlikely to have been caused by the release of natural pain-killing endorphins, which are not very hallucinogenic, or by cerebral hypoxia (low oxygen levels in the brain), which tends to create mental confusion instead of the clarity of thought usually reported. But perhaps most damaging to the argument that NDEs are imaginary rather than actual, is the fact that several subjects recounted meeting people in the afterlife whom they recognized, but who had died, sometimes at a distant place, while they were unconscious, and whose deaths they otherwise could have known nothing about.

Hence heaven and hell *are* realities and it is only our intrinsic selfishness which keeps hell full.

Bibliography

Aelfric, *Homilies*, translated by Benjamin Thorpe (Aelfric Society, 1846)

Apparitions, Supernatural Occurrences, Demonstrative of the Soul's Immortality, from the manuscript of an Eminent Divine (J. Barker, 1799)

Augustine, St, *Concerning the City of God Against the Pagans*, translated by Henry Bettenson (Penguin, 1972)

Baxter, Richard, *The Certainty of the World of Spirits* (Parkhurst & Salusbury, 1691)

Beaumont, John, *An Historical, Physiological and Theological Treatise of Spirits, Apparitions, Witchcrafts, and other Magical Practices* (D. Brown et al. 1705)

Bede, *A History of the English Church and People*, translated by Leo Sherley-Price (Penguin, 1955)

Bettenson, Henry (ed.), *Documents of the Christian Church* (World's Classics, 1943)

Bodin, Jean, *Le Théâtre de la nature universelle*, translated from Latin by M. François de Fougerolles (I. Pillehotte, 1597)

Blackmore, Susan, 'Near-death Experiences' (*Journal of the Royal Society of Medicine*, Vol. 89, February 1996)

Budge, Sir Ernest A. Wallis, *Stories of the Holy Fathers* (Oxford University Press, 1934)

Coles, Harry L., *The War of 1812* (University of Chicago Press, 1965)

Dante, *Divina Commedia*, translated by Revd Henry Francis Cary (George Bell & Sons, 1888)

Davidson, H.R. Ellis, *Gods and Myths of Northern Europe* (Penguin, 1964)

Davies, Rodney, *Buried Alive* (Robert Hale, 1999)

Davies, Rodney, *Doubles: The Enigma of the Second Self* (Robert Hale, 1998)

Erasmus, Desiderius, *Twenty Select Colloquies*, translated by Sir Roger L'Estrange (Chapman & Dodd, undated)

Fenimore, Angie, *My Near-death Journey to the Edge of Hell* (Bantam, 1995)

Fillion, Revd L.C., *The Life of Christ*, translated by Revd Newton Thompson (R. Herder, 1948)

Graves, Robert, *The Greek Myths* (Penguin, 1955)

Gregory, St, *The Dialogues of Saint Gregory, surnamed the Great* (Philip Lee Warner, 1911)

Gregory of Tours, *The History of the Franks*, translated by O.M. Dalton (Oxford, 1927)

Guiberg, Abbot, *The Autobiography of Guibert Abbot of Nogent-Sous-Couc*, translated by G.G. Coulton (George Routledge & Sons, 1925)

Grenside, Dorothy, *The Meaning of Dreams* (G. Bell & Sons, 1923)

Guillaume le Breton, 'Vie de Philippe-Auguste', *Collection des mémoires relatif à l'histoire de France* (Chez J-L-J Brière, 1825)

Hakluyt, Richard, *The Principal Voyages of the English Nation* (J.M. Dent, 1907)

Hare, Augustus, *The Story of My Life* (George Allen, 1900)

Here is a Full and True Relation of One Richard Langly, a Glazier (London, 1708)

Herodotus, *The Histories*, translated by Aubrey de Selincourt (Penguin, 1954)

Hesiod, *Theogony*, translated by Dorothea Wender (Penguin, 1973)

Hill, William, *The Life and Visions of Nicholas Hart* (John Baker, 1711)

Homer, *The Iliad*, translated by E.V. Rieu (Penguin, 1950)

Homer, *The Odyssey*, translated by E.V. Rieu (Penguin, 1955)

The Kentish Wonder or the Wonder of Kent: Being a strange but true account of Mary Stone (C. Wheeler, 1780)

Kerényi, Carl, *The Gods of the Greeks*, translated by Norman Cameron (Pelican, 1958)

Kung, Hans, *Eternal Life? Life after death as a medical, philosophical, and theological problem* (Doubleday, 1984)

James, Montague Rhodes, *The Apocryphal New Testament* (Oxford University Press, 1924)

Jung, Carl, *Memories, Dreams, Reflections* (Fount Paperbacks, 1977)

Laertes, Diogenes, *Lives of the Eminent Philosophers* (William Heinemann, 1928)

Lavaterus, Lewes, of Tigurine, *Of Ghosts and Spirits, Walking by Night*, translated by R.H. (Thomas Creede, 1596)

Lilly, William, *History of His Life and Times* (reprinted for Charles Baldwyn, 1822)

Lund, David H., *Death and Conscious* (McFarland & Company, 1985)

MacKenzie, Donald, *Egyptian Myth and Legend* (Gresham, undated)

Marks, Alfred, *Tyburn Tree, Its History and Annals* (Brown, Langham, undated)

Mead, G.R.S., *Did Jesus Live 100 BC?* (Theosophical Publishing Society, 1903)

Mountague, James, *The Old Bailey Chronicle* (S. Smith, 1788)

N.H., *Ladies' Dictionary; Being a General Entertainment for the Fair Sex* (J. Dunton, 1694)

Orton, Job, *Memoirs of the Life, Character and Writings of the late Philip Doddridge DD of Northampton* (J. Buckland, 1745)

Osis, Karlis, and Erlender, Haraldsson, *At the Hour of Death*, rev. edn. (Hastings House, 1986)

Owens, J.E., Cook, E.W., and Stevenson, I. 'Features of "near-death experience" in relation to whether or not patients were near death' (*The Lancet*, 10 November, 1990)

Paul the Deacon, *History of the Langobards*, translated by William Dudley Foulke (Longmans, Green, 1907)

Plato, *The Republic*, translated by H.D.P. Lee (Penguin, 1955)

Pliny, *Natural History*, translated by John Bostock (Henry G. Bohn, 1855)

Present Day Dreams and Visions, by a Curate (Revd H.W. Bates, 1898)

Robinson, Matthew, *The Wonderful Trance of Matthew Robinson, in his own words* (M. Wright, 1821)

Roger of Wendover, *Flowers of History* (Bohn's Library, 1848)

Sandars, N.K. (trans.) *The Epic of Gilgamesh* (Penguin, 1960)

Saxo Grammaticus, *The First Nine Books of the Danish History of Saxo Grammaticus*, translated by Oliver Elton (David Nutt, 1894)

Simpson, Revd David, *A Discourse on Dreams and Night-Visions* (Edward Bayley, 1810)

Studies in Biology: comprising the Agonies of Hanging, by One Who was Cut Down from the Gallows (William Freeman, 1868)

Swedenborg, Emanuel, *Heaven and Hell* (Swedenborg Society, 1937)

The Trance: a Poem, founded on fact, in which the Author had a vision of Heaven and Hell (printed for the author by H. and I. Gibbon, 1826)

Tregortha, John, *News from the Invisible World; or, Interesting Anecdotes of the Dead* (printed and published by J. Tregortha, 1808)

Tyson, John, *The Lancashire Wonder, being a full account of Mr Jeremiah Carter* (1630)

Virgil, *The Aeneid*, translated by David West (Penguin, 1990)

Watkins, Richard, *Newes from the Dead* (Oxford, 1651)

William of Newburgh, *Historia Rerum Anglicarum*, translated by Revd Joseph Stevenson (*The Church Historians of England*, vol IV, part II, 1856)

Index